MILITARY AIRCRAFT
RECOGNITION

Airlife

Key Recognition Points

To identify the aircraft type refer to the key letters and find possible aircraft by checking against the letter code shown in the contents page.

ENGINES

A PROPELLER

B JET

C WING-MOUNTED

D NOSE-MOUNTED

E WITHIN FUSELAGE

> **Number of Engines**
> 1, 2, 3, 4, or 8

JET INTAKES

G IN WING

H SIDE FUSELAGE

I BENEATH

WINGS

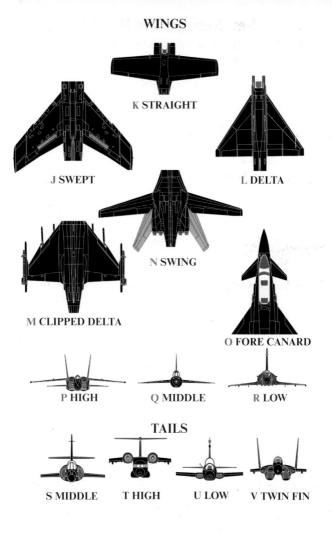

K STRAIGHT

J SWEPT

L DELTA

N SWING

M CLIPPED DELTA

O FORE CANARD

P HIGH

Q MIDDLE

R LOW

TAILS

S MIDDLE

T HIGH

U LOW

V TWIN FIN

Contents

ADA LCA   *India*

On 4 January 2001 the first Full Scale Engineering Development (FSED) example of the ADA LCA (TD-1, above) completed its first flight. The Light Combat Aircraft (LCA) is the result of a programme begun in 1983, in which the Indian government strove to develop an indigenous fourth-generation combat aircraft to replace the MiG-21. Both MBB and Dassault have acted as consultants at one time or another for the project, which is led by the Aeronautical Development Agency (ADA), a division of India's Defence Research and Development Organisation, with Hindustan as lead partner. Initially, the aircraft was supposed to enter service in the mid 1990s, but this soon proved impractical, especially when GE withdrew its support for the F404 powerplant that was chosen to power the development aircraft. Nevertheless, work continued, with the Kaveri engine being tested in Russia during 2001 and due to be fitted in a third FSED aircraft. All of the aircraft's major systems, including its radar and avionics are to be indigenously developed, with up to 80 per cent of the final production aircraft scheduled to be of Indian origin. A series of prototypes will follow the FSED aircraft, these including two-seat training aircraft and a single-seater designed for operation from the Indian navy's new aircraft carrier. It seems unlikely that the LCA will be in service by the ADA's optimistic date of 2006.

LCA (production aircraft)
Powerplant: one GTRE GTX-35VS Kaveri turbofan rated at about 80.45 kN (18,078 lb st) with afterburning

Performance: max speed (estimated) Mach 1.8, service ceiling (estimated) more than 15240 m (50,000 ft)

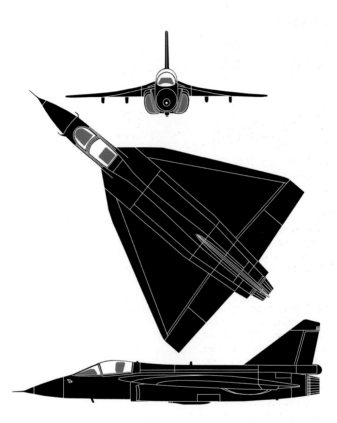

Dimensions: wing span 8.20 m (26 ft 10¾ in), length 13.20 m (43 ft 3¾ in), height 4.40 m (14 ft 5¼ in)

Recognition features
A Delta wing with cranked leading edge
B Single engine
C No canards

Aermacchi MB.339 *Italy*

The success of the MB.326 led Aermacchi to design the MB.339, with a pressurised cockpit, improved canopy, new ejection seats and modified systems. It was powered by an upgraded Rolls-Royce Viper Mk 632-43 and the prototype first flew on 12 August 1976. The Italian Air Force (AMI) ordered a batch of 101 MB.339As to replace MB.326s, first deliveries taking place in 1980, and further orders were received from Argentina, Ghana, Malaysia, UAE, Peru and Nigeria. The MB.339 was unsuccessfully entered in the American JPATS (Joint Primary Aircraft Training System) competition. The single-seat ground-attack MB.339K Veltro II, which has only flown as a development aircraft, had six underwing hardpoints and twin 30-mm DEFA 553 cannon in the forward fuselage. The MB.339CB is an improved MB.339 with a 235-kg (520-lb) gross weight increase, more powerful Viper Mk 680 engine, the MB.339K wing and a HOTAS cockpit management system. Some 18 were sold to New Zealand but have since been retired from service. The MB.339CD (above) has a full digital cockpit and the MB.339FD is a similar lead-in fighter trainer and light ground attack version with increased power.

MB.339FD
Powerplant: one 19.30-kN (4,340-lb st) Rolls-Royce Viper Mk 680-43 turbojet

Performance: max speed 902 km/h (563 mph), max cruising speed 818 km/h (505 mph), initial climb rate 2012 m (6,600 ft) per min, range 1932 km (1,207 miles)

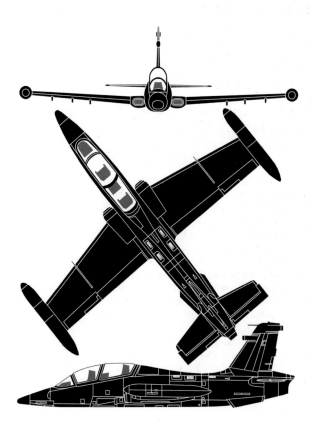

Dimensions: wing span 11.20 m (36 ft 9 in), length 11.24 m (36 ft 10 in), height 3.94 m (12 ft 11 in)

Recognition features

A Low-set wing with tip tanks

B Engine intakes at wing roots

C Long forward fuselage with large single-piece canopy

Aero L-59 and L-159 *Czech Republic*

The Aero L-39 Albatros was succeeded by the L-59 (formerly L-39MS, of which five were delivered to the Czech air force) which first flew on 30 September 1986. This is a higher-performance aircraft with a new turbofan engine developed by ZVL and the Soviet Lotarev bureau, and a strengthened airframe. The L-59 also has a modernised cockpit with a HUD and an improved tactical navigation system. The main production variant has been the L-59E weapons trainer with four underwing hardpoints and a belly-mounted gun pod and 48 of these have been sold to Egypt. Tunisia received 12 of the generally similar L-59T. The Czech air force has ordered 72 of the L-159 ALCA (Advanced Light Combat Aircraft) which is a single-seat close support version with a Honeywell/ITEC F124-GA-100 turbofan. An L-159B two-seater is also offered and expected to form part of the Czech order, although the customer has been frustrated by delays in the programme. Aero Vodochody, as the company is now titled, also entered the JPATS competition with the L-139 Albatros 2000 (above) which was equipped with a Garrett TFE731-4-1T turbofan, but it was unsuccessful in the competition and no production aircraft were built.

L-59 Albatros
Powerplant: one 21.58-kN (4,850-lb st) ZMDB-Progress DV-2 turbofan

Performance: max speed 875 km/h (545 mph), cruising speed 764 km/h (477 mph), initial climb rate 1560 m (5,120 ft) per min, range 1475 km (917 miles) at 5000 m (16,400 ft)

Dimensions: wing span 9.55 m (31 ft 4 in), length 12.20 m (40 ft 1 in), height 4.77 m (15 ft 8 in)

Recognition features

A Low-set, straight wing

B Shoulder-mounted engine air intakes above wing

C Pointed forward fuselage

Aérospatiale SA 341 Gazelle *France*

Sud Aviation's SA 340 light helicopter was required as a replacement for the Alouette II and under Aérospatiale it was developed into the SA 341 Gazelle, the prototype flying on 17 April 1968. The initial customer was the UK, which received 282 Astazou IIIN-powered, Westland-built Gazelle AH.Mk 1, HT.Mk 2, HT.Mk 3 and HCC.Mk 4, helicopters, and ALAT, which received 340 SA 341Fs with Astazou IIIC engines and the later SA 342M (right) dedicated anti-tank model with the larger Astazou XIVH. The type was widely exported and Yugoslavia's Soko built 132 of the SA 341H Partizan helicopter and several SA 342Ms.

Recognition features A Extensive cockpit glazing **B** Fenestron tail rotor **C** Three-bladed rotor

Agusta A129 Mangusta and Scorpion *Italy*

The Mangusta was designed as a state of the art all-weather scout attack helicopter with night operating capability. The A 129 has a fixed tail-wheel undercarriage and two Rolls-Royce Gem turboshafts mounted in pods on either side of the upper fuselage driving a four-bladed composite main rotor. All stores are carried under two stub wings. The Mangusta prototype first flew on 11 September 1983. Agusta has launched the A 129 International (right) with full all-weather capability and LHTEC CTS800-2 turboshafts but none had been sold by early 2002. The A 129 Scorpion is an enhanced version equipped with Hellfire missiles, a three-barrelled 20-mm cannon and enhanced avionics.

Recognition features A Heavily-stepped cockpits **B** Large undernose gun installation **C** Two-bladed tail rotor

Antonov An-12 'Cub' *USSR/Ukraine*

Antonov's An-12 'Cub' freighter was based on the earlier An-10 airframe with an upswept rear fuselage and double ventral loading doors. It retained the An-10's tail turret and glazed nose and was powered by four AI-20M turboprops. The majority of An-12s was delivered to the Soviet air force but exports were made to Bulgaria, Czechoslovakia, Poland and India (right). Many special variants were built and the type is built in China as the Shaanxi Y-8.

Recognition features A Glazed nose **B** Large dorsal fin **C** Portly fuselage

AIDC F-CK-1 Ching-Kuo *Taiwan*

With a well-developed aircraft manufacturing industry in place, Taiwan launched a plan in 1982 to replace its existing Lockheed F-104 Starfighter fleet with a modern interceptor. With technical help from American companies including Lockheed Martin, AIDC (Aerospace Industrial Development Corporation) designed the IDF (Indigenous Defence Fighter) Ching-Kuo. The first Ching-Kuo, a single-seat FSD aircraft (above), flew for the first time on 28 May 1989. The type has been produced in single- (now correctly termed as F-CK-1A) and tandem two-seat (F-CK-1B) versions, and has a digital fly-by-wire control system. Primary air-to-air armament consists of a single M61A Vulcan cannon in the port wing root and wingtip-mounted Sky Sword AAMs. There are four underwing hardpoints and a fuselage centreline mounting for a mixed load of up to 3900 kg (8,600 lb) of disposable ordnance. AIDC built 102 single-seat and 28 two-seat Ching-Kuos, the survivors of which remain in service. AIDC has been seeking an industrial partner in developing a LIFT version of Ching-Kuo and an MLU is also being developed.

F-CK-1A Ching-Kuo

Powerplant: two Honeywell/AIDC TFE1042-70 turbofans each rated at 42.26 kN (9,500 lb st) with afterburning

Performance: max speed 1298 km/h (805 mph), cruising speed 1012 km/h (635 mph), max climb rate at sea level (estimated) 15240 m (50,000 ft) per min, service ceiling 16760 m (55,000 ft), range (estimated) 555 km (345 miles)

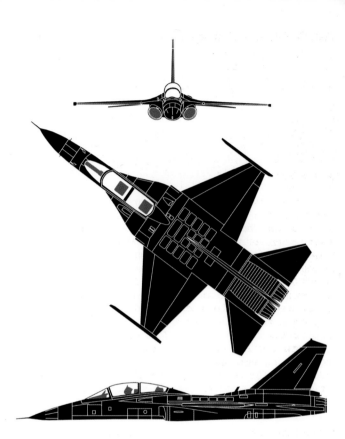

Dimensions: wing span 8.53 m (28 ft), length 14.22 m (46 ft 7 in), height 4.72 m (15 ft 6 in)

Recognition features
A Short-span, tapered, straight wing
B Lateral engine air intakes beneath wing roots
C Twin engines

15

Alenia G222 and C-27J Spartan *Italy*

Originally intended as a standard tactical transport for NATO forces, the G222 was designed by Fiat in 1962 and became primarily an Italian air force project, being first flown at Turin on 18 July 1970. By this time Fiat was part of Aeritalia which then became part of Alenia. The G222 was extensively redesigned, having been planned, initially, with lift jets in the lower engine nacelles and wingtips. The production aircraft was a conventional twin turboprop with 62-troop capacity and a rear loading ramp, and the first of 44 aircraft for the AMI was delivered in 1976. AMI G222s have also been used for airways checking, ECM work and firefighting. Further sales were made to the air forces of Dubai, Argentina, Libya, Nigeria, Thailand, Venezuela and Somalia. Over 100 G222s had been delivered when production ceased in 1989. The C-27A Spartan was a special missions version, ten of which were ordered for the USAF in 1997 from a reopened production line, and the C-27J Spartan, which first flew on 25 September 1999, is a new Lockheed Martin/Alenia development with Rolls-Royce AE2100 engines and upgraded avionics.

G222
Powerplant: two 2535-kW (3,400-shp) Fiat-General Electric T64-GE-P4D turboprops

Performance: max speed 540 km/h (335 mph), cruising speed 440 km/h (275 mph); initial climb rate 520 m (1,700 ft) per min, range 2500 km (1,563 miles)

Dimensions: wing span 28.70 m (94 ft 2 in), length 22.70 m (74 ft 5½ in), height 9.80 m (32 ft 2 in)

Recognition features
A Shoulder-mounted wing
B Twin turboprop engines
C Ramp tail

AMX International AMX   *Italy/Brazil*

Aeritalia/Aermacchi conceived the AMX tactical fighter-bomber/recon-
naissance aircraft in 1979 to replace the Aeritalia G.91 and joined with
EMBRAER in 1980 to produce the aircraft for the Italian and Brazilian
air forces under the AMX International banner. The initial Italian AMX
first flew on 15 May 1984 and the Brazilian prototype (designated
YA-1) on 16 October 1985. The partners subsequently added the
AMX-T (above) (Brazilian TA-1/A-1B) tandem two-seat operational
trainer which maintains the full tactical capability of the standard
AMX. The AMX has four underwing hardpoints, a centreline weapons
station and wingtip mountings for two AIM-9 Sidewinder or MAA-1
Piranha AAMs. The first aircraft entered service in both countries in
1989 and deliveries from the combined manufacturing organisation to
meet Brazil's requirement for an eventual 79 A-1s and 15 A-1Bs
continue, while Italy's purchase of 110 AMXs and 26 AMX-Ts has been
completed. An advanced AMX-MLU has been developed for Brazil and
Italy, the latter planning to bring its surviving single-seaters to this standard. Italian AMXs participated in *Allied Force* in 1999, while eight two-
seat AMX-ATAs, with Elbit avionics, were ordered by Venezuela in
September of the same year.

AMX
Powerplant: one 49.10-kN
(11,030-lb st) Rolls-Royce
RB.168-807 Spey turbofan

Performance: max speed
1047 km/h (654 mph), cruising
speed 960 km/h (600 mph), initial
climb rate 3124 m (10,250 ft) per
min, service ceiling 13000 m
(42,650 ft), range 925 km
(575 miles)

Dimensions: wing span 8.87 m (29 ft 2 in), length 13.23 m (43 ft 5 in), height 4.55 m (14 ft 11 in)

Recognition features

A Mid-set, swept wing

B Large, high-set cockpit enclosure

C Mid-set engine air intakes for single engine

Antonov An-26, An-30 and An-32 *Ukraine*

The An-24 (ASCC/NATO reporting name 'Coke') found limited military use as a personnel transport, but provided an ideal basis for further development, and its first major new version was the An-26 'Curl' which appeared in 1969. It is a cargo-carrying aircraft with the basic An-24 structure but with an upswept rear fuselage incorporating a loading ramp and with two large ventral strakes. It has a hardened militarised freight fuselage without windows, and is fitted with a floor freight handling system and loading hoist. The An-26 is also used for electronic intelligence tasks and can carry bombs on external fuselage mountings. The type is built in China, the military variants under the Xian Y7H series of designations, while the electronic variants were given the NATO designation 'Curl-B'. For passenger transport, up to 40 seats can be fitted. Total production is reported as 1,398. It was followed by the An-32 'Cline' which is based on the An-26, but optimised for 'hot and high' operations with AI-20DM Srs. 5 engines in deep nacelles set above the wing. Approximately 350 had been built by early 2002. The An-30 'Clank' is a specialised An-26 variant for survey and mapping with a fully glazed nose and belly-mounted cameras. It is in use by the Czech air force for Open Skies monitoring (above). Only the An-32 remains in production by Antonov.

An-32 'Cline'

Powerplant: two 3812 kW (5,112 shp) ZMD Progress AI-20DM Srs. 5 turboprops

Performance: max speed 530 km/h (329 mph), cruising speed 470 km/h (292 mph), take-off run 760 m (2,495 ft), landing run 470 m (1,542 ft), service ceiling 9500 m (31,170 ft), range 2000 km (1,250 miles)

Dimensions: wing span 29.20 m (95 ft 9 in), length 23.78 m (78 ft), height 8.75 m (28 ft 8 in)

Recognition features
A High-set wing
B Ramp tail with prominent ventral strakes
C An-32 engines mounted above wing

Antonov An-70 *Ukraine*

With an ageing fleet of An-12s in service with civil and military operators worldwide, Antonov started design work in 1987 on a new propfan-powered freighter, designated An-70, for civil and military applications. This was a larger aircraft with more than double the gross weight of the An-12 but it followed the familiar Antonov high-wing layout with a ventral rear loading ramp and externally podded main undercarriage fairings. Unlike previous freighters, the An-70 has a fully pressurised cargo area and is fitted with a powered loading system including travelling cranes and a rollamat floor. The D-27 propfan engines are fitted with counter-rotating propellers with curved composite blades. The An-70 prototype first flew on 16 December 1994 but was destroyed in February 1995 in a collision with an An-72 chase aircraft. The second prototype then took over the test programme. On 2 April 2001 the Ukrainian government finally signed an order for the first five of its total requirement for 65 An-70s. Production is scheduled for the Aviant factory in Kiev and the Aviakor facility at Samara, and should begin during 2002. An order from the Russian air force seems unlikely in the near future.

An-70
Powerplant: four 10440-kW (14,000-shp) Ivchenko-Progress/ Zaporozhye D-27 propfan engines

Performance: max speed 797 km/h (495 mph), cruising speed 741 km/h (460 mph), take-off run 1800 m (5,900 ft), landing run 2200 m (7,220 ft), range 4900 km (3,063 miles)

Dimensions: wing span 44.06 m (144 ft 7 in), length 40.70 m (133 ft 8 in), height 16.38 m (53 ft 9 in)

Recognition features
A Multi-bladed 'propellers' on propfan engines
B Classic transport layout
C Distinctive sound

Antonov An-28 and An-38   *USSR/Poland*

In 1969 the first prototype of the turboprop An-28 'Cash' was flown as a light transport. The production version was built by PZL-Mielec. A batch of SAR An-28B1Rs (right) was delivered to the Polish navy. A new version with PT6A engines, the M-28 Skytruck, has since entered production. The latest version is the stretched An-38-100 which first flew on 23 June 1994. Powered by TPE331-14GR turboprops it will be built in the Ukraine. **Recognition features A** Strut-braced high-aspect ratio wing **B** Twin fins **C** Fixed tricycle undercarriage

Bell 209 HueyCobra and SuperCobra   *USA*

The Model 209 (AH-1) HueyCobra combined the engine and rotor system of the UH-1C with a new fuselage, stub wings and a chin-mounted gun turret. The prototype first flew on 7 September 1965 and initial US Army AH-1G deliveries were made in June 1967. Later variants included the USMC's AH-1J SeaCobra with a PT6T-3 TwinPac powerplant and the AH-1S (right). The AH-1W SuperCobra has two T700-GE-401 turboshafts, a three-barrelled 20-mm cannon and Hellfire missile capability. The AH-1Z is an upgraded AH-1W with four-bladed rotors. **Recognition features A** Stepped tandem cockpits **B** Very narrow slab-sided fuselage **C** Two-bladed rotors on most models

Boeing AH-64 Apache   *USA*

Designed as the Hughes Model 77, the YAH-64A first flew on 30 September 1975. It is a two-seat aircraft with a slim fuselage, a prominent fin with a low-mounted elevator and stub wings. Twin T700-GE-701 turboshafts are employed. The production AH-64A (right) has an under-fuselage-mounted M230 Chain Gun and can carry up to 16 AGM-114A Hellfire ATGMs. The AH-64D Longbow Apache, which first flew on 15 April 1992 has a mast-mounted Longbow radar, more power, enlarged fuselage side fairings and more sophisticated avionics. The AH-64D is in production and being produced by upgrade. It is also being built by Westland as the WAH-64D Apache AH.Mk 1, powered by RTM322 engines, for the British Army. **Recognition features A** Stepped tandem cockpits with flat glazing **B** Tall air-data sensor of radome above main rotor **C** Non-perpendicular tail rotor blades

Antonov An-72 & 74 'Coaler'   *Ukraine*

Antonov's small turbofan freighter, the An-72 'Coaler' (above), was first flown on 31 August 1977. It embodies a number of highly innovative features, the principal one being the mounting of its two D-36 turbofans above and forward of the wing centre section. This results in STOL performance as a result of the jet exhaust blowing over the wing surface and giving improved lift coefficients. The An-72 has a rear loading ramp, T-tail and externally podded main landing gear. Military variants are legion and include the An-71 with a fuselage-mounted tailplane and a forward-swept fin with a large rotodome on top for AEW&C tasks; the An-72S VIP transport; An-72V for export and An-72P maritime patrol aircraft. The latter is equipped with a twin-barrelled 23-mm cannon in a pod on the starboard side of the fuselage, as well as underwing rocket pods as standard. It can also drop four bombs from the cabin roof above the rear ramp, the latter being slid away to allow the bombs to be dropped. The An-74 was originally developed as a specialised Arctic-support version with increased fuel capacity and other changes, although the designation has now come to apply to civil versions in general. In excess of 160 An-72/An-74 aircraft have been completed and the type remains in production. A revised design, known as the An-74-300, or An-174 in stretched form, has its engines in underwing nacelles.

An-72 'Coaler-C'
Powerplant: two 63.74-kN (14,330-lb st) Lotarev D-36 turbofans

Performance: max speed 705 km/h (438 mph), cruising speed 598 km/h (374 mph), take-off run 930 m (3,050 ft), landing run 465 m (1,525 ft), service ceiling 11800 m (38,715 ft), range 4800 km (3,000 miles)

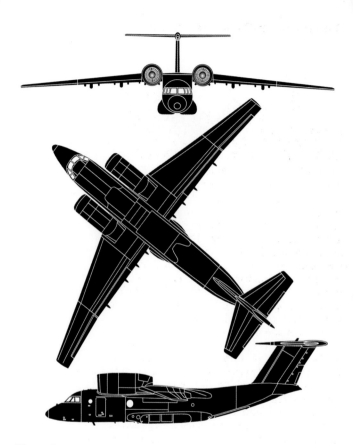

Dimensions: wing span 31.90 m (104 ft 7 in), length 28.07 m (92 ft 1 in), height 8.65 m (28 ft 4 in)

Recognition features
A Twin turbofan engines mounted above and ahead of wings
B Upswept ramp rear fuselage
C Straight wings with swept leading edge

BAe Sea Harrier

The BAe P.1184 Sea Harrier FRS.Mk 1 was a dedicated carrier-based version of the RAF's Harrier GR.Mk 3, developed for the Royal Navy and first flown on 20 August 1978. It differed from the GR.Mk 3 in having a revised forward fuselage with a raised cockpit canopy and a pointed radome containing Blue Fox radar. The Sea Harrier also had a 95.57-kN (21,490-lb st) Pegasus Mk 104 engine and some structural modifications for the naval role. Some 57 Sea Harriers (and four two-seat Harrier T.Mk 4N trainers) were delivered to the Royal Navy and the Indian Navy acquired 23 single-seat Sea Harrier FRS.Mk 51s and four two-seat Harrier T.Mk 60s. The Sea Harrier FRS.Mk 2 (later designated FA.Mk 2) is an upgraded version of the earlier Sea Harrier with Blue Vixen radar in a larger nose radome, improved systems with a modernised cockpit, a lengthened rear fuselage and a Pegasus Mk 106 engine. The radar is one of the most capable fighter radars extant and provides full AMRAAM compatibility. The Sea Harrier is to be retired in 2004-6 and replaced by the GR.Mk9 in 2007. Some 35 Harrier FRS.Mk 1s were modified to FA.Mk 2 standard and 18 new aircraft were also built.

Sea Harrier FA.Mk 2
Powerplant: one 95.60-kN (21,500-lb st) Rolls-Royce Pegasus Mk 106 vectored-thrust turbofan

Performance: max speed 1185 km/h (735 mph), cruising speed 972 km/h (608 mph), max climb rate at sea level about 15240 m (50,000 ft) per min, range 185 km (115 miles) for a 1 hour 30 min CAP

Dimensions: wing span 7.70 m (25 ft 3 in), length 14.17 m (46 ft 6 in), height 3.60 m (11 ft 10 in)

Recognition features

A Four exhaust nozzles beneath wing roots

B High-set, anhedralled wing

C Unusual radome shape

BAE Systems Hawk *UK*

Hawker Siddeley (later British Aerospace, then BAE Systems) designed the HS.1182 Hawk to replace the Folland Gnat T.Mk 1, which was the standard RAF jet trainer in the 1960s. The Hawk has a tandem two-seat cockpit, low wing and single Adour turbofan. It is larger than the Gnat, so offering the RAF greater flexibility and weapons-carrying potential. The initial Hawk T.Mk 1 was first flown on 21 August 1974 and RAF deliveries started in mid-1976. Hawks have been acquired by 16 overseas countries including Abu Dhabi (Mk 63A), Australia (Mk 127), Canada (Mk 115), Finland (Mk 51), Indonesia (Mk 53), South Korea (Mk 67), Saudi Arabia (Mk 65) and Switzerland (Mk 66). Local assembly has been carried out in Finland and Switzerland. In the US, the Hawk was adopted by the US Navy as its standard advanced trainer as the much modified T-45A Goshawk. Some 189 examples will be delivered, production by McDonnell Douglas commencing in 1988 and continuing, as the T-45C, with Boeing. The Hawk 200 is a single-seat combat version which has been sold to Indonesia, Malaysia (Srs 208), Saudi Arabia (Srs 205) and Oman (Srs 203). The prototype first flew on 19 May 1986. BAE Systems also offers the Hawk 100 (above) improved version of the T.Mk 1, with modified wings incorporating wing tip Sidewinder rails and a longer nose incorporating a FLIR sensor.

Hawk T.Mk 1
Powerplant: one 23.10-kN (5,200 lb st) Rolls-Royce/ Turboméca Adour 151-01 turbofan

Performance: max speed 990 km/h (615 mph), max cruising speed 928 km/h (580 mph), initial climb rate 3600 m (11,800 ft) per min, range 2895 km (1,810 miles)

Dimensions: wing span 9.39 m (30 ft 9 in), length 10.77 m (35 ft 4 in), height 3.98 m (13 ft)

Recognition features
A Low-set, swept wing
B Mid-set engine air intakes ahead of wing
C Large canopy over raised cockpit line

BAE Systems Nimrod

The Nimrod maritime reconnaissance and anti-submarine warfare aircraft was based on the de Havilland Comet 4C four-jet airliner from which it differed principally in having a shorter fuselage with a lower lobe added to house a large weapons bay, a redesigned vertical tail with a tip-mounted antenna, a MAD boom extending from the rear fuselage and a large nose radome to house a search radar. The prototype first flew on 23 May 1967 and the first of 46 Nimrod MR.Mk 1s, powered by four Spey turbofans, entered service with the RAF in 1969. The surviving fleet of 35 aircraft was upgraded to MR.Mk 2 standard from 1980 with new radars and equipment and later, beginning during the Falklands War, as MR.Mk 2Ps (above) with in-flight refuelling probes and tail finlets. The RAF also operates three Nimrod R.Mk 1 (R.Mk 1P when refuelling probes were added, although the 'P' was later dropped for both the R.Mk 1 and MR.Mk 2) intelligence-gathering aircraft which lack the MAD tail boom and have wing-mounted electronics pods in place of the external wing tanks, as well as a plethora of fuselage antennae. It is intended that the Nimrod will be upgraded to Nimrod 2000 (MRA.Mk 4) standard with Rolls-Royce Deutschland BR710 turbofans and a new mission system, with 21 aircraft being converted by 2008.

Nimrod MR.Mk 2
Powerplant: four 54-kN (12,140-lb st) Rolls-Royce RB.168-20 Spey Mk 250 turbofans

Performance: max speed 925 km/h (575 mph), cruising speed 880 km/h (545 mph), take-off distance 1462 m (4,800 ft), range 9600 km (6,000 miles)

Dimensions: wing span 35 m (114 ft 10 in), length 38.60 m (126 ft 9 in), height 9.08 m (29 ft 9 in)

Recognition features
A Sloping cockpit and nose profile, with probe above
B Double engine air intakes at wing roots
C Double-lobe fuselage

Bell Boeing V-22 Osprey *USA*

Bell and Boeing established the joint Osprey project in 1982 in response to the Joint Services Advanced Vertical Lift programme which covered a wide performance envelope and multiple tasks. The resultant V-22 was based on the tilt-rotor concept tested earlier by Bell on its XV-15 which had first flown in early 1977. The Osprey has a conventional transport aircraft fuselage, largely built from composites, with a ventral rear loading ramp and the ability to carry 24 troops or 12 stretcher cases. The wing is mounted on top of the fuselage and has a complex flap/aileron system and two tip-mounted swivelling pods housing the Rolls-Royce turboshafts, which are fitted with large, three-bladed proprotors. The XV-22A prototype first flew on 19 March 1989, followed by nine proto-type and development aircraft. The USAF will receive CV-22B special missions aircraft, the USMC will receive MV-22B assault transports and the USN will take HV-22B CSAR/fleet logistics aircraft.

CV-22A Osprey
Powerplant: two 4586-kW (6,150-shp) Rolls-Royce T406-AD-400 turboshafts

Performance: max level speed at sea level 509 km/h (316 mph), max cruising speed at sea level as a helicopter 185 km/h (115 mph), max vertical climb rate at sea level 332 m (1,090 ft) per min, range with no payload 3892 km (2,418 miles)

Dimensions: wing span 15.52 m (50 ft 11 in), length 17.47 m (57 ft 4 in), height 5.38 m (17 ft 7 in)

Recognition features
A Twin turboshafts mounted at wingtips
B Tiltrotor configuration
C Large-diameter proprotors

Boeing Helicopters CH-47 Chinook USA

The CH-47 Chinook first flew in August 1959, with twin T55 turboshafts mounted on the outside of the tail pylon. The first example of the definitive US Army CH-47A was handed over in August 1962 and the design was progressively improved as the CH-47B and CH-47C. Upgraded and new build CH-47D-standard helicopters (right) are now in widespread service, as are special operations versions including the MH-47E. Export customers include the RAF and the CH-47 has been built under licence in Italy and Japan.

Recognition features A Large fuselage side sponsons **B** Fixed four-leg undercarriage **C** Twin rotors **D** Engines in pods on rear rotor pylon

Boeing Sikorsky RAH-66 Comanche USA

Boeing has joined with Sikorsky to develop the RAH-66 Comanche two-seat armed reconnaissance helicopter to replace the US Army's OH-58s and some AH-64s. The project was initiated in late 1990 and two proto-types and five EMD helicopters will be built. The YRAH-66 was first flown on 4 January 1996 but funding delays have slowed the programme. The aircraft is 'stealthy', largely built from composites and has fly-by-wire control systems. The twin LHTEC turboshafts are buried in the centre fuselage and are heavily shrouded for IR protection.

Recognition features A Angular shape **B** Fenestron tail rotor **C** Retractable undercarriage

Cessna A-37B Dragonfly USA

The Cessna T-37C export jet trainer was built with light attack capability and this formed the basis for the YAT-37D close air support prototype first flown on 22 October 1963. The A-37 Dragonfly has a further strengthened wing with three hardpoints on each side, wing tip tanks as standard, cockpit armour plating, self-sealing fuel tanks and new avionics. It has J85 turbojets and the production A-37B (right) has a flight-refuelling probe and a nose-mounted GAU-2B/A Minigun. It was pressed into service by the USAF and VNAF in Vietnam and many were exported. Chile, Guatemala, Peru, Uruguay and Colombia still operated the type in 2002.

Recognition features A Straight, low-set wings **B** Side-by-side, two-seat cockpit **C** Short undercarriage

Boeing B-52H Stratofortress *USA*

As the key element of the USAF strategic nuclear bombing force for over 45 years, the B-52 Stratofortress has a commanding place in history. This large swept-wing bomber, now only operating in its later B-52H form, was designed by Boeing in 1949 and first flown on 2 October 1952. The B-52H is stressed for low-altitude operations and can carry up to eight AGM-86 cruise missiles internally and 12 on external pylons. Other weapons include the full range of Mk 80-series dumb bombs, cluster bombs, JDAM and AGM-142 Have Nap. The type's tail-mounted Vulcan cannon has long since been deleted, in favour of advanced ECM systems. Low-level penetration is aided by low-light level TV and FLIR systems housed in chin turrets. Between 1954 and 1962 a total of 744 B-52s was built. Approximately 85 remain in front-line USAF service and such is the B-52's versatility that it is expected to remain in service until at least 2040. Various upgrades are planned and re-engining schemes have been mooted. The B-52D, -52F and -52G served over Vietnam, while the B-52G flew during *Desert Storm* in 1991. The B-52H has seen combat over the Balkans, during Operation *Desert Fox* and most recently during Operation *Enduring Freedom* over Afghanistan.

B-52H Stratofortress

Powerplant: eight 75.60-kN (17,000-lb st) Pratt & Whitney TF33-P-3 turbofans

Performance: max speed 952 km/h (595 mph), cruising speed 816 km/h (510 mph), take-off run 2896 m (9,500 ft), service ceiling 17765 m (55,000 ft), range 12000 km (7,500 miles)

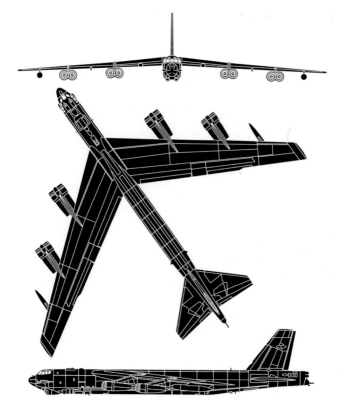

Dimensions: wing span 56.39 m (185 ft), length 49.05 m (160 ft 11 in), height 12.40 m (40 ft 8 in)

Recognition features
A Eight engines in four paired cowlings
B Long narrow fuselage
C Unique undercarriage layout

Boeing C-17A Globemaster III

USA

The C-17A strategic airlifter, now in service with the USAF, was designed to the 1980 C-X specification and its fuselage and tail design owes much to the smaller YC-15 transport built by McDonnell Douglas in 1975. The C-17A has a classic cargo transport layout with a ventral rear fuselage loading ramp, shoulder wing with a blown flap system, T-tail and externally podded main undercarriage bogies. It is designed for operation by three crew and is powered by four PW2040 (F117-PW-100) turbofans in wing-mounted pods. The Globemaster III, which first flew in prototype form on 15 September 1991, can carry complex loads including the M1 Abrams main battle tank or three Bradley infantry vehicles and RAH-66 or AH-64 helicopters. Alternatively, it can carry up to 102 troops or 48 stretcher cases. It not only has good STOL characteristics for tactical delivery but also has transcontinental range for strategic supply missions. The first USAF squadron became operational in January 1995 and 70 of the initial procurement of 120 C-17As had been delivered by mid-2000. Some 13 further machines have been ordered for delivery from 2004 and funding for a further 15 C-17As has been granted. Up to 12 more may be requested in 2003. Four leased aircraft are in RAF service.

C-17A Globemaster III
Powerplant: four 179.70-kN (40,400-lb st) Pratt & Whitney PW2040 turbofans

Performance: max speed 941 km/h (585 mph), cruising speed 901 km/h (560 mph), take-off run 2359 m (7,740 ft), service ceiling 13715 m (45,000 ft), range 10000 km (6,250 miles)

Dimensions: wing span 51.76 m (169 ft 10 in), length 53.03 m (174 ft), height 16.79 m (55 ft 1 in)

Recognition features
A Classic transport layout
B Tall winglets
C T-tail with narrow-chord fin

41

Boeing E-3 Sentry

The success of the Boeing 707 as a military platform for a huge range of tasks made it the natural choice as the basis for an AWACS (Airborne Warning and Control System). The 707-320B airframe, powered by Pratt & Whitney TF33-PW-100 turbofans, was modified with a large twin-pylon-mounted 9-m (30-ft) diameter rotodome fitted to the upper rear fuselage for the large Westinghouse downlook radar. Internally, the aircraft accommodates 18 mission crew whose consoles and equipment are served by a powerful CC-2 computer. The E-3 (initially EC-137D) prototype first flew on 5 February 1972 and 34 have been delivered to the USAF, while 18 were received by NATO. The USAF E-3As have been replaced by E-3B and E-3C aircraft with improved APY-2 radar. Four E-3Fs have been sold to France, the RAF operates seven E-3D Sentry AEW.Mk 1s (above) and the Royal Saudi Air Force has five E-3As. All three of these latter models are fitted with CFM56-2A-3 engines and the NATO E-3s may be upgraded to this standard. The 17 surviving NATO aircraft have been updated with the AN/AYR-1 ESM system, which adds distinctive radomes either side of the nose. Saudi Arabia received eight KE-3A tankers based on the E-3 airframe and has since added a KE-3B 707 conversion.

E-3A Sentry

Powerplant: four 93.40-kN (21,000-lb st) Pratt & Whitney TF33-PW-100A turbofans

Performance: max speed 848 km/h (530 mph), cruising speed 816 km/h (510 mph), initial climb rate (estimated) 457 m (1,500 ft) per min, operating ceiling 8840 m (29,000 ft), range 4800 km (3,000 miles)

Dimensions: wing span 44.40 m
(145 ft 9 in), length 46.60 m
(152 ft 11 in), height 12.70 m
(41 ft 9 in)

Recognition features
A Huge pylon-mounted rotodome
above rear fuselage
B Low-set, swept wing
C Four turbofan engines

Boeing F-15 Eagle _USA_

Now in front-line operation for almost 30 years, the F-15 has given excellent service with the USAF and other air forces and is only now reaching the end of its production life with about 1,500 aircraft having been built. First flown on 27 July 1972, the Eagle has appeared in fighter and attack variants. The first of the fighters was the F-15A, which introduced the type's standard air-to-air configuration of four AIM-9 Sidewinders and drop tanks on two underwing pylons, and four AIM-7 Sparrows on fuselage hardpoints, with provision for a tank on the centreline. It is also equipped with a 20-mm M61A Vulcan cannon. The F-15B is the combat-capable tandem two-seat trainer version of the F-15A. The F-15C (and two-seat F-15D), which first flew in February 1979, have improved radars and engines, and can be fitted with conformal fuel tanks (CFTs) on the fuselage sides. Mitsubishi builds the F-15J (F-15C) and F-15DJ for the JASDF. The F-15E (originally named Strike Eagle) (above) is a two-seat ground attack version. It has 12 CFT ordnance stations, in addition to its two wing and one centreline pylon, and also carries LANTIRN navigation and targeting pods. Variants for Israel and Saudi Arabia are referred to as the F-15I and F-15S.

F-15E Eagle
Powerplant: two Pratt & Whitney F100-P-229 turbofans each rated at 129.40 kN (29,100 lb st) with afterburning

Performance: max speed more than 2655 km/h (1,650 mph) at altitude, initial climb rate (estimated) 18593 m (61,000 ft) per min, service ceiling 18290 m (60,000 ft), range 4416 km (2,760 miles)

Dimensions: wing span 13.05 m (42 ft 10 in), length 19.43 m (63 ft 9 in), height 5.61 m (18 ft 5 in)

Recognition features

A Twin vertical fins

B Large semi-delta wing

C Sharply raked, rectangular-section engine air intakes

Boeing F/A-18 Hornet   *USA*

Derived from the Northrop YF-17 light fighter design, the F/A-18 Hornet was designed for the US Navy as a carrier-based fighter and attack aircraft. The prototype first flew on 18 November 1978 with first deliveries of the F/A-18A (and tandem two-seat F/A-18B) taking place in 1979. The Hornet is a semi-delta design with twin vertical fins and nine external weapons stations and it is powered by two 71.15-kN (16,000-lb st) F404-GE-400 (later -402) afterburning turbofans. It is fitted with wing folding and arrester gear for carrier operations. The F/A-18C (and two-seat F/A-18D), which commenced deliveries in 1994, is an upgraded F/A-18A with new AN/APG-73 radar and systems to allow operation of AIM-120 AMRAAM. It also has enhanced night operational capability through use of the externally carried Nite Hawk targeting system. The F/A-18E (and two-seat F/A-18F, above) Super Hornet is a substantially improved version, now in production, which has increased wing span and fuselage length, a higher useful load providing increased fuel capacity and greater range, and improved combat damage resilience. The EA-18 Growler is a jamming variant intended as a replacement for the EA-6B Prowler. In addition to the US Navy and US Marine Corps, users include Australia (AF-18A and ATF-18A), Canada (CF-188A/B), Finland, Kuwait, Malaysia, Spain (EF-18A/B designated C.15 and CE.15) and Switzerland. Brazil and Kuwait have shown interest in the F/A-18E/F.

F/A-18E Super Hornet
Powerplant: two General Electric F414-GE-400 turbofans each rated at 97.87-kN (22,000-lb st) with afterburning

Performance: max speed 2221 km/h (1,380 mph), max cruising speed 1287 km/h (800 mph), combat ceiling 15240 m (50,000 ft), range 3312 km (2,070 miles)

Dimensions: wing span 13.61 m (44 ft 8 in), length 18.31 m (60 ft 1 in), height 4.88 m (16 ft)

Recognition features
A Twin outward-canted fins
B Twin engine air intakes beneath wing leading edge root extensions
C Rectangular intakes under enlarged LERXes on E/F

CASA C.212 Aviocar   *Spain*

In 1969, CASA started work on the C.212 light utility STOL transport, primarily to meet a Spanish air force requirement. The high-wing Aviocar has a square-section fuselage, fixed tricycle undercarriage and an upswept rear fuselage incorporating a loading ramp. It is powered by two wing-mounted TPE331 turboprops and has 19 seats in passenger configuration. The first C.212-100 (above) flew for the first time on 26 March 1971 and 79 were delivered to the Spanish air force under the designation T.12B (or TR.12A for survey work and TE.12B as dual control trainers). The C.212-200 is a higher-powered version with TPE331-5 engines; the C-212-300 has TPE331-10R-513C engines, winglets and a lengthened nose; and the C-212-400 has TPE331-12 engines and a higher useful load. The C-212-300M is the military variant of the -300. Special missions variants of the -300/-400 are available for ASW or MP work and these are marketed under the name Patrullero. The C.212 has been built under licence by IPTN in Indonesia as the NC.212, and deliveries have been made to military and civil customers including the air forces of Mexico, Zimbabwe, Panama, Angola, Argentina and Bolivia and air carriers such as Pelita Air Services, Korean Air and Merpati Nusantara. CASA is now an EADS company.

C.212-300
Powerplant: two 671-kW
(900-shp) Honeywell
TPE331-10R-513C turboprops

Performance: max speed
370 km/h (230 mph), cruising
speed 354 km/h (220 mph), initial
climb rate 95 m (312 ft) per min,
range 1422 km (890 miles)

Dimensions: wing span 20.28 m (66 ft 6 in), length 16.15 m (53 ft), height 6.60 m (21 ft 8 in)

Recognition features
A High wing
B Square-section, boxy fuselage
C Large fin fillet

CASA C-295 *Spain*

Airtech was formed in 1982 by CASA and IPTN to develop the CN-235 medium transport. A larger aircraft than the earlier C.212 Aviocar, it has a circular-section fuselage incorporating a rear loading ramp and external fairings to accommodate the fully retractable undercarriage. The majority of the 241 aircraft ordered by June 2000 were for military users as the CN-235M (known as the Tetuko in Indonesia). These include the air forces of Chile, France, Spain, Indonesia, Ireland and Saudi Arabia. Aircraft for the Turkish air force are being licence-built in Turkey. The Spanish prototype flew on 11 November 1983 and initial production CN-235-10 aircraft had CT7-7A engines. The later CN-235-100 has more powerful CT7-9C turboprops. The CN-235-200 has a strengthened airframe, modified wing and increased fuel load; and the CN-235-300 has a glass cockpit, in-flight refuelling capability and improved pressurisation. An MP variant, designated CN-235MPA, has been sold to Brunei, Indonesia and Spain. CASA has also developed the C-295 (above) independently from Airtech. This aircraft, which first flew on 28 November 1997, has a stretched fuselage giving a 50 per cent increase in capacity, Pratt & Whitney Canada PW127G engines and six-bladed propellers. It has been delivered to the Spanish air force and is on order for Poland.

CN-235-100
Powerplant: two 1305-kW (1,750-shp) General Electric CT7-9C turboprops

Performance: max speed 445 km/h (276 mph), cruising speed 423 km/h (265 mph), initial climb rate 465 m (1,525 ft) per min, service ceiling 6860 m (22,500 ft), range 835 km (522 miles)

Dimensions: wing span 25.80 m (84 ft 8 in), length 21.40 m (70 ft 2 in), height 8.18 m (26 ft 10 in)

Recognition features
A Classic transport layout, with pointed forward fuselage and extensive cabin glazing
B Large sponsons for main U/C
C Strake beneath fin

Dassault Super Etendard

France

The Dassault Etendard IVM single-seat naval strike fighter entered service with the Aéronavale in 1962. The low-wing Etendard was designed for French Navy carrierborne strike operations and 90 were delivered. On 29 October 1974, Dassault flew the prototype of the follow-on Super Etendard, modified from an Etendard IVM, with a higher-thrust Atar 8K-50 engine and a new radar and attack system. The Aéronavale received 71 Super Etendards, with first deliveries taking place in 1978. Fourteen aircraft were delivered to the Argentine Navy (above) and flown in the Falklands War, while five were leased to Iraq and used in the first Gulf War. The Super Etendard is equipped with two internal DEFA 553 30-mm cannon and can carry a variety of offensive stores including two Exocet or R.550 Magic missiles on its four under-wing hardpoints and centreline stores station. Production was completed in 1983. French Super Etendards have been the subject of upgrading, the first of these schemes adding a stand-off nuclear strike capability with the ASMP (Air-Sol Moyenne Portée) missile and various avionics modifications. A further upgrade, carried out in the light of delays to the Rafale M programme, raised the Super Etendards to Modernisé standard. This in itself is being further improved, and the type is not expected to retire until around 2010.

Super Etendard
Powerplant: One 49-kN (11,025-lb st) SNECMA Atar 8K-50 turbojet

Performance: max speed 1200 km/h (750 mph), cruising speed 1088 km/h (680 mph), initial climb rate 6096 m (20,000 ft) per min, service ceiling more than 13700 m (44,950 ft), combat radius 850 km (528 miles) for an anti-ship mission

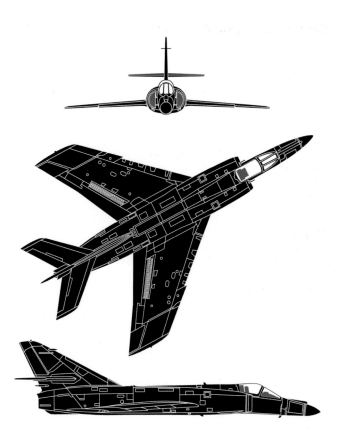

Dimensions: wing span 9.60 m (31 ft 6 in), length 14.31 m (46 ft 11 in), height 3.86 m (12 ft 8 in)

Recognition features
A Long drooped nose profile
B Low-set wing and mid-set tailplane
C All flying surfaces swept

Dassault Mirage 2000 *France*

For the third of its Mirage family, Dassault restored the delta wing layout and wing-mounted undercarriage of the Mirage III/5/50. This was combined with a slightly larger area-ruled fuselage and an M53 turbofan. Armament consists of two DEFA 554 belly-mounted cannon and external weapons on four wing hardpoints and five underfuselage pylons. The Mirage 2000 prototype flew for the first time on 10 March 1978. Basic variants are the 2000C (above) all-weather interceptor, 2000B two-seat trainer, 2000N nuclear strike aircraft and the similar 2000D conventional ground attack variant. The Mirage 2000-5 is a specialised export model with upgraded avionics and weapons integration, and provision for MICA air-to-air missiles, and the Mirage 2000-5 Mk 2 and 2000-9 are variants with further improvements to their datalink system, a new ECM system, Damocles laser designator, increased gross weight and a redesigned modular cockpit. Some 37 Armée de l'Air Mirage 2000Cs have been upgraded to Mirage 2000-5F standard equivalent to the 2000-5 export machines. The aircraft has been widely exported and has seen combat during *Desert Storm*, over the Balkans (where a Mirage 2000D was lost) and over Afghanistan. Over 600 Mirage 2000s are in service.

Mirage 2000C
Powerplant: one SNECMA M53-P2 turbofan rated at 95.10 kN (21,385 lb st) with afterburning

Performance: max speed 2300 km/h (1,437 mph), cruising speed 1400 km/h (875 mph), initial climb rate 16765 m (55,000 ft) per min, range 1840 km (1,150 miles)

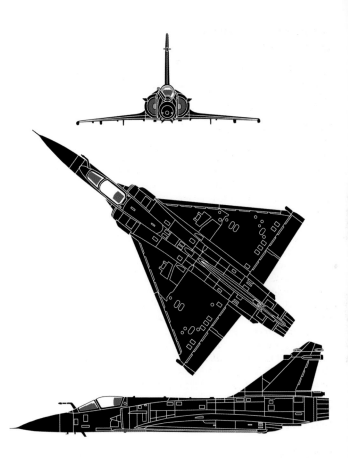

Dimensions: wing span 9.13 m (29 ft 11 in), length 14.36 m (47 ft 1 in), height 5.20 m (17 ft 1 in)

Recognition features
A Tailless delta configuration
B Single engine
C Long conical radome

Dassault Rafale *France*

In 1984 Dassault started development work on a new twin-engined multi-role fighter to meet the needs of the French air force and navy, and the proof-of-concept Rafale A first flew on 4 July 1986. The definitive production Rafale, which flew in May 1991, is slightly smaller. It is a delta-winged aircraft, built with advanced material and powered by twin M88 turbofans mounted in the lower fuselage. It is fitted with moving canards positioned beside the cockpit. Variants for l'Armée de l'Air are the Rafale C single-seater and Rafale B two-seater. The Aéronavale is to receive the Rafale M (above) which is a navalised carrierborne version with modified twin-wheel nose gear, long-stroke main undercarriage legs and an arrester hook. The aircraft has six underwing hardpoints, two wingtip missile stations and five underfuselage pylons, together with an internal 30-mm cannon. Four prototypes were used for flight testing and the first of 61 initial production aircraft flew in December 1998. The anticipated French military requirement is for 234 Rafales.

Rafale C

Powerplant: two SNECMA M88-2 turbofans each rated at 72.90 kN (14,400 lb st) with afterburning

Performance: max speed 2125 km/h (1,321 mph), cruising speed 1012 km/h (633 mph), initial climb rate around 18288 m (60,000 ft) per min, service ceiling 16765 m (55,000 ft), range 3680 km (2,300 miles)

Dimensions: wing span 10.80 m (35 ft 5 in), length 15.27 m (50 ft 1 in), height 5.34 m (17 ft 5 in)

Recognition features
A Canards
B Delta wing

Dassault (Breguet) Atlantique   *France*

Avions Louis Breguet designed the Atlantic as a replacement for the Lockheed Neptune which was the standard postwar NATO long-range maritime reconnaissance type. The Atlantic prototype first flew on 21 October 1961. Production was a French, German, Dutch and Belgian project with final assembly handled by Breguet at Biarritz. The twelve-crew Atlantic was delivered to the French Aéronavale (40), Italy (18), the Netherlands (9) and the German Kriegsmarine (20), the latter having modified five for Elint missions. Pakistan received three ex-French machines. The Br.1150 Atlantic has a large belly weapons-bay capable of carrying bombs, depth charges and up to eight torpedoes, and four underwing hardpoints. It is equipped with ASW avionics and a Thomson search radar. The Dassault Atlantique ATL (Atlantic Nouvelle Génération) 2 (above), 30 of which have been sold to the Aéronavale, is an upgraded version with completely new electronic equipment including wingtip-mounted ESM and a Tango FLIR in a nose housing. The proposed ATL 3 would have Rolls-Royce AE2100 turboprops and a new mission system, while a Europatrol version has been suggested as a replacement for NATO Orions.

Atlantique 2
Powerplant: two 4549-kW (6,100-shp) Rolls-Royce Tyne RTy.20 Mk 21 turboprops

Performance: max speed 648 km/h (403 mph), cruising speed 556 km/h (345 mph), initial climb rate 610 m (2,000 ft) per min, service ceiling 9145 m (30,000 ft), range 7,778 km (4,861 miles)

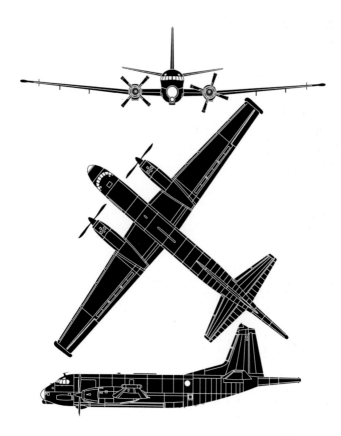

Dimensions: wing span 37.46 m (122 ft 11 in), length 31.72 m (104 ft 1 in), height 11.30 m (37 ft 1 in)

Recognition features
A MAD boom at tail
B Twin turboprop engines
C Distinctive fin shape; dihedralled tailplane

Dassault/Dornier Alpha Jet *France/Germany*

The Alpha Jet was the result of one of the earliest European cooperative defence aircraft projects. Its aim was to create an advanced jet trainer for the French and German air forces. The Alpha Jet is a tandem two-seat aircraft with a shoulder-mounted swept wing and two lower fuselage-mounted Larzac turbofans. The prototype flew for the first time on 26 October 1973 and the initial variants were the Alpha Jet E (above) trainer and Alpha Jet A light attack variant, the latter with a belly-mounted cannon pod and four underwing hardpoints, for the Luftwaffe. Some 447 Alpha Jets were delivered, including aircraft for Belgium and the Ivory Coast. Egypt received 45, designated MS1 and MS2, of which 37 were built by the Helwan factory, and Cameroon received seven tactical support variants similar to the Egyptian MS2. The Alpha Jet NGEA (Nouvelle Génération Ecole/Appui; later Alpha Jet 2) was proposed as a new weapons-training version with Larzac 04-C20 engines but none have been ordered to date.

Alpha Jet E
Powerplant: two 13.24-kN (2,976-lb st) Turboméca/SNECMA Larzac 04-C6 turbojets

Performance: max speed 1000 km/h (621 mph), cruising speed 960 km/h (597 mph), take-off run 370 m (1,215 ft), initial climb rate 3657 m (12,000 ft) per min, service ceiling 14630 m (48,000 ft), range 2880 km

(1,800 miles)
Dimensions: wing span 9.11 m (29 ft 11 in), length 11.75 m (38 ft 7 in), height 4.19 m (13 ft 9 in)

Recognition features
A Shoulder-mounted wing with pronounced anhedral
B One exhaust nozzle on each side of rear fuselage
C Large multi-section cockpit enclosure

EMBRAER Tucano/Super Tucano   *Brazil*

Brazilian air force needs for a new advanced trainer resulted in EMBRAER developing the turboprop EMB-312 Tucano which first flew on 16 August 1980. The Tucano is of all-metal construction with a low wing and tandem two-seat cockpit, and is powered by a 559-kW (750-shp) Pratt & Whitney Canada PT6A-25C turboprop. Both the student (in the front seat) and instructor sit on ejection seats. In Brazilian air force service it is designated T-27 and sales have also been made to Argentina; Honduras; Iran; Paraguay; Peru; Venezuela and to France, as the EMB-312F with additional airbrakes. The Tucano has been licence-built in Egypt for Egypt and Iraq and 131 were built for the Royal Air Force by Shorts at Belfast as the S-312 Tucano T.Mk 1 with an 820-kW (1,100-shp) Garrett TPE331-12B turboprop and a modified cockpit canopy. Shorts also delivered aircraft to Kenya and Kuwait. The EMB-312H (later EMB-314) Super Tucano (above) has a 1.37-m (4-ft 6-in) fuselage stretch, a PT6A-68 engine, enlarged cockpit canopy and upgraded systems, while the ALX armed version with five hardpoints is being built as the AT-29 and single-seat A-29 for the Brazilian air force. In addition, on 20 August 2001, the Dominican Republic signed an order for ten export-standard ALXs.

EMB-312H Super Tucano
Powerplant: one 1193-kW (1,600 shp) Pratt & Whitney Canada PT6A-68-1 turboprop

Performance: max speed 556 km/h (346 mph), cruising speed 530 km/h (330 mph), initial climb rate 895 m (2,935 ft) per min, take-off run 350 m (1,150 ft), range 1557 km (974 miles)

Dimensions: wing span 11.14 m (36 ft 6 in), length 11.43 m (37 ft 6 in), height 3.90 m (12 ft 9 in)

Recognition features
A Raised cockpit and large canopy over wing roots
B Tall, narrow-chord fin
C Five-bladed propeller

Eurofighter Typhoon *International*

The high-technology Eurofighter, or EF2000 or Typhoon, is under development by BAE Systems (UK), Daimler Chrysler Aerospace (Germany), Alenia (Italy) and CASA (Spain). Seven development prototypes, including two two-seaters, have flown, the first on 27 March 1994. Eurofighter is a twin-turbofan, multi-role combat aircraft for close-in combat, ground attack, air interdiction and air defence beyond visual range and has limited stealth characteristics. It is delta-winged with a forward canard surface and conventional vertical fin, and is built in single-seat and tandem two-seat versions, both of which are fully combat capable and fitted with 13 external stores stations and a 27-mm Mauser cannon. Initial orders are for 620 aircraft for the four partner countries with service entry scheduled for 2002. The Eurofighter is equipped with fly-by-wire and advanced management systems, the latter including a head-up display, helmet-mounted display and voice-activated controls. It is named Eurofighter 2000 for use by the participating nations and Typhoon for the RAF and export sales. The Spanish air force designates the aircraft C.16, in single-seat form, and CE.15 (above). Greece has pledged to sign a 60-aircraft order after the 2004 Olympic Games.

Typhoon
Powerplant: two Eurojet EJ200 turbofans each rated at 90 kN (20,250 lb st) with afterburning

Performance: max speed 2435 km/h (1,522 mph), take-off run for an air-to-air mission 300 m (985 ft), radius for a single-seat low altitude ground attack mission 601 km (374 miles)

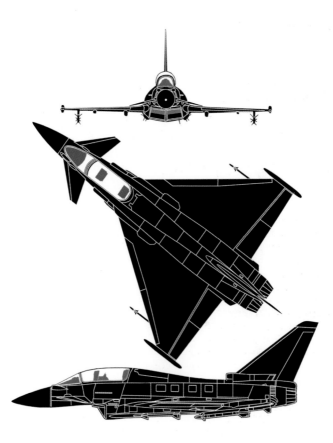

Dimensions: wing span 10.95 m (35 ft 11 in), length 15.96 m (52 ft 5 in), height 5.28 m (17 ft 4 in)

Recognition features
A Twin engine air intakes beneath forward fuselage
B Anhedralled canards
C Delta wing

EH Industries EH 101   *Italy/UK*

The European Helicopter Industries partnership between Westland and Agusta was formed in 1980 to develop the EH 101. The EH 101 is a medium-lift helicopter powered by three General Electric CT7-2A or Rolls-Royce/Turboméca RTM322 turbines mounted above the fuselage. The initial EH 101 flew for the first time on 9 October 1987. Military variants include the RTM322-powered Merlin HM.Mk 1 for the Royal Navy (right), the RAF's Merlin HC.Mk 3 and the Cormorant SAR helicopter for the Canadian Armed Forces. Military EH 101s are also on order for Denmark, Italy and Portugal. **Recognition features A** Triple engines **B** Retractable U/C **C** Five-bladed main rotor

Eurocopter Cougar   *France*

The SA 330 Puma was first flown on 14 April 1965. Over 700 were built before production switched to the AS 332 Super Puma. This has a longer forward fuselage, ventral tail fin, a new rotor head and Makila engines. In 1990 military Super Pumas were redesignated as AS 532 Cougars (right). Further improvement led to the stretched AS 532 Cougar 2 being flown in prototype form on 6 February 1987. The AS 532U2 and A2 Cougar 2 remain in production in 2002, as does the EC 725 Cougar 2+.
Recognition features A Four-bladed main rotor **B** Boxy fuselage **C** Retractable U/C

Eurocopter EC 665 Tiger   *France/Germany*

The Tiger was the second of the jointly developed helicopters produced by Aérospatiale and MBB following the formation of Eurocopter. The Tiger is a tandem two-seat all-weather combat helicopter which will be produced in UHT combat/support, HAP escort/support (right) and HAC anti-tank versions. Built largely of composites, it is an all-weather aircraft with advanced avionics and weapons systems. It can fire Stinger AAMs and HOT-2 and TRIGAT anti-tank missiles. The first Tiger was flown at Marignane on 27 April 1991. The Tiger (Tigre in France) has been ordered by Australia, Germany and France.
Recognition features A Stepped, angular cockpit enclosures **B** Tall mid-fuselage section **C** Tail fins

FMA IA-63 Pampa

Argentina

The Pampa was designed by the Argentine state military aircraft factory FMA in cooperation with Dornier, as a primary and advanced jet training aircraft to replace the Argentinian air force's Morane-Saulnier MS.760s. The Pampa design followed the lines of the Alpha Jet and other jet trainers, with a tandem-seat layout and retractable tricycle undercarriage. The shoulder wing is of low aspect ratio with no sweep and equal taper, and the Pampa is powered by a TFE731 turbofan. The Pampa prototype made its first flight on 6 October 1984. The production Pampa, which entered service in 1988, is fitted with five weapons hardpoints and standard equipment includes a centreline podded DEFA cannon to allow the aircraft also to be used for ground attack. Only 19 Pampas were delivered to the Argentinian air force, but FMA, now owned by Lockheed Martin and trading as Lockheed Martin Aircraft Argentina SA, delivered one further aircraft in 1999 and production of a further batch of 12 has been initiated. A Pampa 2000 International version was unsuccessful in the JPATS competition, while advanced Naval, Pampa NG A and combat-capable NG B variants have been proposed. Elbit avionics are being used to upgrade 12 Argentinian Pampas.

IA-63 Pampa
Powerplant: one 15.57-kN (3,500-lb st) Honeywell TFE731-2-2N turbofan

Performance: max speed 821 km/h (510 mph), cruising speed 748 km/h (465 mph), initial climb rate 1561 m (5,120 ft) per min, service ceiling 12900 m (42,320 ft), take-off run 420 m (1,380 ft), range 1487 km (930 miles)

Dimensions: wing span 9.69 m (31 ft 9 in), length 10.93 m (35 ft 10 in), height 4.29 m (14 ft 1 in)

Recognition features
A High-set, straight wing
B Stepped shape to lower rear fuselage
C One-piece cockpit canopy

Grumman F-14 Tomcat

USA

The design of the F-14 Tomcat resulted from the failure in the mid-1960s of the F-111B to meet a US Navy specification. Grumman's F-14 was primarily designed as an air superiority fighter with the ability to carry substantial ordnance for the ground attack role. First flown on 21 December 1970 the F-14 has a tandem two-seat cockpit, twin Pratt & Whitney TF30 reheated turbofans and variable-sweep wings. The tail unit consists of twin fins and all-moving elevators and the Tomcat is fitted with a tricycle undercarriage and arrester hook. Hardpoints are fitted under the wing gloves but the main load of Sparrow or Phoenix missiles is carried on fuselage-mounted pylons and on suitably modified aircraft a Tactical Air Reconnaissance Pod System (TARPS) pod can be carried. Hardpoints beneath the engine nacelles can carry long-range fuel tanks. The F-14A (above) remains in service with the Iranian air force and the US Navy, while the latter also flies the re-engined F-14B and F-14D. Most recently the F-14 has seen combat in its new 'Bombcat' role, as a long-range attack aircraft over the Balkans and Afghanistan. The US Navy is looking to accelerate F-14 retirement in favour of the F/A-18E/F.

F-14A Tomcat
Powerplant: two Pratt & Whitney TF30-P-414A turbofans each rated at 92.97 kN (20,900 lb st) with afterburning

Performance: max speed 2485 km/h (1,544 mph), cruising speed 982 km/h (610 mph), initial climb rate 9906 m (32,500 ft) per min, range 3,840 km (2,400 miles)

Dimensions: wing span 19.54 m (64 ft 1½ in) spread, length 19.10 m (62 ft 8 in), height 4.88 m (16 ft)

Recognition features
A Twin vertical fins
B VG wings
C Huge wing gloves on upper fuselage

Ilyushin Il-76 'Candid' *Russia*

The Il-76 (ASCC/NATO codename 'Candid') freighter, which made its first flight on 26 March 1971, is the standard CIS medium-/heavy-cargo carrier for civil and military applications. Complementing or replacing the An-12 in service, the Il-76 is a pressurised aircraft with an anhedralled high-set wing mounting four podded D-30 turbofans. The wing is mounted on top of the fuselage to give an unobstructed internal load compartment with clamshell rear loading doors below the rear fuselage. The Il-76 has a glazed nose housing a navigator's station and many aircraft have a tail turret. Production of the Il-76 exceeds 920 aircraft and variants include the Il-76T with increased fuel capacity and the Il-76TD with D-30KP-1 engines. Many Il-76s have been delivered for military use as the Il-76M and have been widely modified as airborne command posts, inflight-refuelling tankers (Il-78 'Midas'), etc. More than 40 Il-76-based AEW aircraft have been built by Beriev as the A-50 'Mainstay' with a pylon-mounted rear fuselage rotodome and associated radar and sensors. A pair of similar-looking aircraft for range support duties was built under the designation Be-976. The Il-76MF (above) has a 6.63-m (21-ft 8-in) fuselage stretch, increased range and four 156.90-kN (35,275-lb st) Aviadvigatel PS-90AN turbofans.

Il-76TD 'Candid-A'
Powerplant: four 117.69-kN (26,455-lb st) Aviadvigatel D-30KP-1 turbofans

Performance: max speed 850 km/h (528 mph), cruising speed 756 km/h (470 mph), take-off run 1700 m (5,580 ft), landing run 1000 m (3,280 ft), range with a 20000-kg (44,090-lb) payload 7300 km (4,535 miles)

Dimensions: wing span 50.49 m (165 ft 8 in), length 46.58 m (152 ft 10 in), height 14.76 m (48 ft 5 in)

Recognition features
A Undernose glazing and radome
B T-tail with large bullet fairing
C No inflight-refuelling receptacle above forward fuselage

ENAER T-35 Pillán   *Chile*

The Pillán is the result of cooperation between ENAER and Piper to produce a basic trainer for the Chilean air force. Piper's XBT prototype which first flew on 6 March 1981 combined a PA-28 Warrior wing with a cut-down version of the PA-32R Saratoga fuselage incorporating a tandem two-seat cockpit with a large bubble canopy. Designated PA-28R-300, it was powered by a 224-kW (300-hp) piston engine. ENAER built 105 T-35 Pilláns from Piper kits, including 80 for Chile (right), ten for Panama (T-35D) and 15 for Paraguay. Another 41 were built by CASA for the Spanish air force as the E.26 Tamiz.

Recognition features A Piston engine **B** Swept fin **C** Retractable undercarriage

Fairchild Republic A-10 Thunderbolt II   *USA*

The A-10 is a specialised ground attack and close support aircraft designed to the requirements of the USAF. The single-seat A-10A has a distinctive layout with two General Electric TF34 turbofans mounted side-by-side on the rear fuselage and first flew in prototype form on 10 May 1972. The wing has fairings to house the retracted main undercarriage and is fitted with 11 hardpoints to carry a variety of ordnance. The A-10 has a nose-mounted 30-mm GAU-8A Avenger cannon. One two-seat YA-10B was tested in 1979. Over 350 remain in active service, some as OA-10A FACs (right). **Recognition features A** Twin fins **B** Two podded turbofans on rear fuselage **C** Straight wing

HAL ALH   *India*

The 12-seat ALH (Advanced Light Helicopter) has been designed by Hindustan Aeronautics Limited with assistance from MBB. It is powered by twin 746-kW (1,000-shp) Turboméca TM 333-2B turboshafts mounted above the cabin to drive a four-bladed composite main rotor. The military prototype first flew on 28 May 1994. The naval version has a folding tail boom, folding rotor blades, external stores-capable sponsons, a retractable tricycle undercarriage and increased gross weight. Development is continuing with first deliveries having been made.

Recognition features A Prominent twin fins **B** Streamlined forward fuselage shape **C** Four-bladed main rotor

Kaman H-2 Seasprite   *USA*

In 1956 Kaman designed a new long-range helicopter for the US Navy. The H-2 Seasprite has a four-bladed main rotor and a tapered fuselage with a vertical tail pylon mounting a tail rotor, and a retractable main undercarriage. It first flew on 2 July 1959. A maximum of two crew and 12 passengers can be carried, but an anti-submarine operations crew of three is more usual. The UH-2A Seasprite was initially powered by a single 652-kW (875-shp) General Electric T58-GE-6, but most aircraft were subsequently modified to twin-turbine UH-2C configuration with a pair of T58-GE-8Bs. Several modification programmes have been implemented including the LAMPS I conversion to SH-2D standard and the upgrade to SH-2F with new rotor blades, modified undercarriage and 1007-kW (1,350-shp) T58-GE-8F engines. The SH-2G Super Seasprite is a refurbished SH-2F with composite rotor blades and twin T700s. Many USN Seasprites have been retired, but surplus SH-2Fs are being rebuilt as SH-2Gs, and new airframes manufactured, for export to Australia, Egypt (above), Poland, New Zealand and possibly Mexico.

SH-2G Super Seasprite
Powerplant: two 1285-kW (1,723-shp) General Electric T700-401 turboshafts

Performance: max speed 270 km/h (168 mph), cruising speed 222 km/h (138 mph), initial climb rate 716 m (2,350 ft) per min, maximum range 885 km (500 miles)

Dimensions: main rotor diameter 13.51 m (44 ft 4 in), length 12.19 m (40 ft), height 4.58 m (15 ft)

Recognition features

A Fuselage-mounted retractable main undercarriage

B Podded engines beneath rotor

C Angled auxiliary fin at base of main fin trailing edge

Lockheed C-5 Galaxy

The C-5 Galaxy is the largest aircraft in the USAF inventory and is used as a strategic airlifter capable of carrying major equipment such as the CH-47 Chinook helicopter and M1A1 Abrams main battle tank, or up to 363 passengers in high-density seating. In general layout, the Galaxy is similar to the C-141 StarLifter but it is 50 per cent larger and can carry more than two-and-a-half times the payload. It has through-loading with a ventral rear ramp and an upward-opening visor nose section and a 24-wheel main undercarriage composed of four separate six-wheel bogies with (on the C-5A) a crosswind landing compensation system. Standard accommodation for five flight crew is provided on an upper deck which can also carry 73 passengers. A total of 77 C-5As was rewinged between 1981 and 1987, with a wing of almost completely new design, giving the aircraft a 30,000-hour life extension. The Galaxy first flew on 30 June 1968 and, between 1969 and 1989, 131 were delivered including 50 C-5Bs with improved systems. The 50 C-5Bs are likely to be re-engined with 266.82-kN (60,000 lb st) General Electric CF6-80C2L1F turbofans from 2007, with an option to modify the rest of the fleet. The C-5 is scheduled for service at least into 2040.

C-5B Galaxy
Powerplant: four 191.26-kN (43,000-lb st) General Electric TF39-GE-1C turbofans

Performance: max speed 917 km/h (570 mph), cruising speed 837 km/h (520 mph), initial climb rate 526 m (1,725 ft) per min, range 10411 km (6,469 miles) with maximum fuel

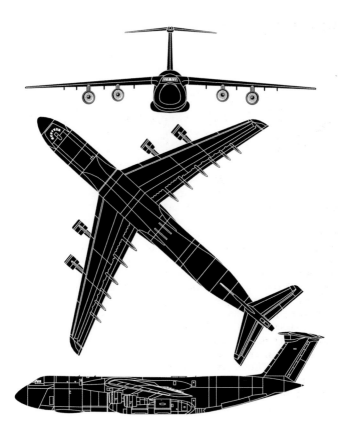

Dimensions: wing span 67.89 m (222 ft 9 in), length 75.54 m (247 ft 10 in), height 19.86 m (65 ft 2 in)

Recognition features
A Huge size
B Bluff, rounded nose shape
C Classic transport layout

Lockheed C-130 Hercules   *USA*

The Hercules has become standard equipment with many of the world's air forces. Designed for the USAF, the C-130 is a high-wing, four-turbo-prop freighter with a loading ramp under the rear fuselage and retractable tricycle landing gear with the main units housed in external fuselage fairings. The prototype flew on 23 August 1954 and the initial C-130As were delivered to the USAF in 1956. Later variants included the C-130B (and US Navy C-130F), the C-130E long-range model, the C-130H with 3026-kN (4,508-shp) T56-A-15s and the similar C-130K for the RAF. Most of these variants spawned special sub-types such as the AC-130A gunship, HC-130B SAR aircraft, MC-130E for special operations, KC-130F aerial refuelling tanker and a range of EC-130E and EC-130H electronic surveillance and airborne communications aircraft. The VC-130H was a VIP transport variant for Saudi Arabia with a luxury interior and square cabin windows. Lockheed also offered stretched -30 variants, and a batch of 30 RAF C-130Ks was upgraded to this standard. The new-generation C-130J was launched in 1991 in standard and stretched C-130J-30 versions. First flown on 5 April 1996, the C-130J has six-bladed propellers, greater range, higher speeds, an advanced two-crew cockpit with new mission computers and avionics, and updated systems.

C-130J-30 Hercules
Powerplant: four 3424-kW (4,591-shp) Rolls-Royce AE2100D3 turboprops

Performance: max speed 644 km/h (400 mph), cruising speed 620 km/h (385 mph), initial climb rate 640 m (2,100 ft) per min, range 5216 km (3,260 miles)

Dimensions: wing span 40.41 m (132 ft 7 in), length 34.36 m (112 ft 9 in), height 11.81 m (38 ft 9 in)

Recognition features
A Classic transport layout
B Prominent 'Roman nose' radome
C Tapered vertical fin

Lockheed F-104 Starfighter *USA*

The F-104 was designed as a high-performance, lightweight, air superiority fighter for the USAF. In the event, its service with the USAF was less significant than its use by other countries. The prototype made its maiden flight on 4 March 1954. The main production models were the F-104G and recce RF-104G, which were designed for NATO in Europe and built by Lockheed, Fiat, Fokker, MBB, and SABCA. In total 1,316 were completed together with 220 TF-104G trainers. The F-104G was also built by Canadair as the CF-104 and CF-104D and by Mitsubishi as the F-104J. The F-104S was an Aeritalia-built dual-purpose ground-attack/air superiority variant for the Italian air force and remained in Italian service in 2002 as the upgraded F-104S ASA (right) and ASA-M.

Recognition features A Slim, pointed fuselage **B** Very short-span wings **C** T-tail

Lockheed U-2 *USA*

The U-2 is notable for the shooting down of Francis Gary Powers over the USSR in May 1960. The prototype U-2A first flew on 4 August 1955. The U-2B and U-2C were upgraded U-2As and the U-2D was a tandem two-seat high-altitude research version. The U-2R (right) was 30 per cent larger and was first flown in 1967 with wing-mounted sensor pods and increased internal provision for sensors. The related TR-1A (later reverting to U-2R) was a tactical recce version. A small number of TR-1B and U-2RT trainers was built and other versions include the ER-2 for NASA research. In-service aircraft in 2002 had been re-engined and were designated U-2S.

Recognition features A Very long-span, high aspect-ratio wings **B** Bicycle undercarriage **C** Equipment pods on wings

Lockheed C-141 StarLifter *USA*

The C-141 StarLifter first flew on 17 December 1963. Powered by four TF33-P-7 turbofans, the C-141A entered service in April 1965. A major upgrade resulted in 271 aircraft being modified as stretched C-141Bs and these continue in wide-scale use, but will eventually be replaced by C-17s.

Recognition features A Classic transport layout **B** Narrow-chord engine nacelles **C** T-tail with narrow-chord fin

Lockheed F-117 Nighthawk   *USA*

The F-117A Nighthawk 'stealth fighter' is a product of the Lockheed 'Skunk Works' at Palmdale, California. Its very low radar signature is achieved by a multi-faceted airframe design and specialised surface coatings, together with careful heat emission shrouding of the jet exhausts. Development started in 1976 and the resultant aircraft has fly-by-wire controls, a highly swept wing integrated with the fuselage to give a continuous dart shape, swept twin ruddervators and a variety of broken edge surfaces to disrupt radar energy reflections. It has two belly weapons bays to carry, most usually, GBU-27 Paveway III laser-guided bombs, although Texas Instruments AGM-88 HARM or Raytheon AGM-65 Maverick air-launched missiles may also be carried. The definitive F-117A prototype first flew on 18 June 1981, with initial operational deliveries being made in 1982. Six YF-117A prototypes and 58 production F-117As have been delivered and the type has been operationally deployed, with great effect, by the 49th Fighter Wing in Operation *Desert Storm* and in the 1999 Kosovo campaign, although in the latter one aircraft was shot down.

F-117A Nighthawk
Powerplant: two 48.04-kN (10,800-lb st) General Electric F404-GE-F1D2 turbofans

Performance: max speed (estimated) 1215 km/h (755 mph), cruising speed (estimated) 1102 km/h (685 mph), initial climb rate 2012 m (6,600 ft) per min, combat radius with maximum weapons 1112 km (691 miles)

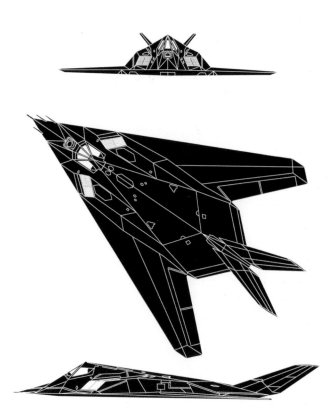

Dimensions: wing span 13.20 m (43 ft 4 in), length 20.09 m (65 ft 11 in), height 3.78 m (12 ft 5 in)

Recognition features
A Unique angular configuration
B Twin outwardly-canted fins
C Sharply swept wings

Lockheed P-3 Orion

USA

Lockheed's L-188 Electra provided an ideal basis for the development of a new maritime patrol aircraft to replace the ageing Lockheed Neptune. The P3V-1 (later YP-3A) Orion, which first flew on 25 November 1959, had virtually the same airframe as the Electra but the cabin windows were deleted and it was fitted with an extended MAD tail boom, a large nose radar, three stores hardpoints on each outer wing panel and a large belly weapons bay to carry torpedoes, mines, bombs and other equipment. Its engines were 3356-kW (4,500-shp) T56-A-10W turboprops. The fuselage was packed with operator consoles for the various detection systems and the rear fuselage housed the aircraft's store of droppable sonobuoys. The P-3A entered US Navy service in 1962 and other users included Canada (CP-140 Aurora), Chile, Holland, Norway, Japan and Pakistan. The P-3B has uprated T56-A-14 engines, the P-3C (above) has an improved suite of ASW equipment and has undergone several subsequent updates, and export models include the P-3F (Iran), P-3K (New Zealand), P-3N (Norway) P-3P (Spain) and P-3W (Australia). The P-3A(CS) is an airborne surveillance version for the US Customs Service with a rotating dish antenna mounted above the fuselage. Many other Orion variants have appeared, including hurricane hunters for the NOAA and Elint EP-3 Aries aircraft.

P-3C Orion

Powerplant: four 3660-kW (4,910 shp) Rolls-Royce T56-A-14 turboprops

Performance: max speed 764 km/h (475 mph), cruising speed 612 km/h (380 mph), patrol speed 381 km/h (237 mph), initial climb rate 594 m (1,950 ft) per min, service ceiling 8625 m (28,300 ft), range 7625 km (4,766 miles)

Dimensions: wing span 30.38 m (99 ft 8 in), length 35.61 m (116 ft 10 in), height 10.29 m (33 ft 9 in)

Recognition features
A Low wing with four turboprops in long nacelles
B Rounded fin top and large fin fillet
C ASW variants have long MAD boom at tip of rear fuselage

Lockheed S-3 Viking

USA

The Viking is the standard US Navy carrier-based anti-submarine warfare aircraft. It is a high-wing machine with folding wing and vertical tail surfaces, twin TF34 turbofans in pylon-mounted underwing pods and a retractable tricycle undercarriage, the main units of which retract into fuselage bays. It has two belly weapons bays to carry up to four Mk 50 torpedoes and two wing hardpoints for fuel tanks or ordnance. The S-3 has a crew of four and is equipped with extensive search and attack avionics including a retractable MAD tail boom. The prototype first flew on 21 January 1972 and the first S-3A operational deliveries took place in 1974. Lockheed has also produced the US-3A COD (carrier on-board delivery) transport. Some 119 Vikings were upgraded to S-3B (above) standard with enhanced offensive electronics and provision for Harpoon missiles, while a further 16 aircraft were converted as ES-3A Shadows for ECM missions. Although it offered a range of extremely useful capabilities, the ES-3A has subsequently been retired from service, the S-3B looking set to follow its example at an accelerated rate. For the time being the S-3 is flying in a number of special roles, some of them experimental and involving advanced ASW and surveillance systems, as well as performing land attack and inflight-refuelling tanker duties.

S-3B Viking
Powerplant: two 41.26-kN (9,275-lb st) General Electric TF34-GE-2 turbofans

Performance: max speed 813 km/h (505 mph), patrol speed 296 km/h (184 mph), initial climb rate 1310 m (4,300 ft) per min, service ceiling more than 10670 m (35,000 ft), range 3440 km (1,870 miles)

Dimensions: wing span 20.93 m (68 ft 8 in), length 16.26 m (53 ft 4 in), height 6.93 m (22 ft 9 in)

Recognition features
A Short fuselage with large cockpit enclosure
B Disproportionately tall fin
C Shoulder-mounted long wing, with twin podded turbofans

Kamov Ka-27, -29, -31 and -32   *Russia*

The Ka-25 coaxial twin-rotor naval helicopter provided the basis for the larger Ka-27 'Helix'. Following the same layout, the Ka-27 prototype first flew on 8 August 1973 and deliveries of the ASW Ka-27PL-O 'Helix-A' to Soviet Naval Aviation started in 1977. Export versions are designated Ka-28. The Ka-27PS 'Helix-D' is a SAR version, while the derived civil Ka-32 has spawned the police Ka-32A-2 and MP Ka-32A-7 (Ka-327). Kamov also developed the Ka-29 army assault helicopter, first flown on 28 July 1976, which has a wider forward fuselage and external armament racks. The Ka-29RLD 'Helix-B' (Ka-31, right) is a radar picket with large forward fuselage housings containing an extendible E-801 flat sensor array. Several air arms use this series of helicopters and a small batch of Ka-29s is being built under licence in India.

Recognition features A Twin, inward-toed fins **B** Stalky undercarriage **C** Co-axial rotor

Kamov Ka-50 and Ka-52   *Russia*

The Ka-50 Black Shark (also named Werewolf) was designed to meet a Soviet requirement for a dedicated single-seat anti-armour helicopter. It is highly manoeuvrable and has a conventional fuselage with a retractable tricycle undercarriage, stub wings and two Klimov TV3-117VMA turboshafts. The Ka-50 'Hokum-A' (right) is the single-seater and first flew on 17 June 1982. The Ka-50N is a night-attack variant, and the Ka-52 Alligator 'Hokum-B' is a side-by-side two-seat all-weather version. **Recognition features A** Tall fin and rudder **B** Twin fins **C** Co-axial rotors

LET L-410 and L-420   *Czech Republic*

LET designed the L-410 Turbolet as a replacement for the Il-12 and flew the prototype XL-410 on 16 April 1969. The production L-410A seats 19 passengers in an unpressurised main cabin. It is powered by two PT6A-27 engines. The L-410M (right) was soon introduced with Motorlet M601A turboprops. The stretched L-410UVP was the main production version. The later L-410UVP-E has wingtip tanks, and the L-420 is a westernised version. **Recognition features A** High wing **B** Pointed nose **C** Tall fin with mid-set tailplane

Lockheed Martin F-16 Fighting Falcon *USA*

The F-16 is the current standard NATO single-seat all-weather multi-role combat aircraft and has been exported globally. It was developed by General Dynamics as a lightweight aircraft to complement the F-15 and the prototype first flew on 21 January 1974. The F-16 has a slim delta wing with a large fairing into the forward fuselage and a conventional all-moving tailplane. A distinctive feature is the large engine air intake on the underside servicing a single reheated turbofan. The F-16 has an internal 20-mm Vulcan cannon. The first F-16A deliveries were made in 1979 together with batches of F-16B tandem two-seat conversion trainers. The F-16 has also been built in Belgium by SABCA, in Holland by Fokker, in Korea by Samsung and in Turkey by TAI. Variants include the F-16A/B (ADF) Air Defence Fighter with its radar modified to provide illumination for AIM-7 Sparrows and the F-16C (above) (and two-seat F-16D), with improved all-weather radar and, later LANTIRN. Early F-16Cs were delivered with Pratt & Whitney F100-PW-200 engines, but from F-16C/D Block 32 standard onwards either the F-100-PW-200 or General Electric F110-GE-100 could be specified. Many in-service F-16s are undergoing various levels of MLU, while USAF F-16C/D Block 50/52 aircraft have systems allowing the use of AGM-88 HARMs in the Wild Weasel role and are unofficially designated F-16CJ/DJ.

F-16C Block 50

Powerplant: one Pratt & Whitney F100-PW-229 turbofan rated at 129.40 kN (29,100 lb st) with afterburning

Performance: max speed 2446 km/h (1,520 mph), initial climb rate (estimated) 15240 m (50,000 ft) per min, range 3872 km (2,420 miles)

Dimensions: wing span 9.45 m
(31 ft), length 15.04 m (49 ft 4 in),
height 5.08 m (16 ft 8 in)

Recognition features
A Oval engine air intake beneath
forward fuselage
B High-set, 'bubble' canopy
C Large fin fillet

Lockheed Martin F-22 Raptor   *USA*

The F-22A advanced single-seat air superiority fighter is under development by Lockheed Martin and Boeing for 2005 service introduction as an F-15 replacement for the USAF. The first of two prototypes was flown on 29 September 1990. The aircraft has an unusual layout to provide significant stealth characteristics with triangular-shaped wings, twin vertical fins and an all-moving tailplane set well back on the fuselage, and is designed for great agility. The Raptor has ventral and side weapons bays to accommodate AAMs, and has an internal M61A2 20-mm Vulcan cannon. It will also be equipped with the 454-kg (1,000-lb) GBU-32 JDAM guided bomb for precision all-weather attack missions. The aircraft is designed to supercruise at speeds up to Mach 1.5 without the use of afterburner. On 19 September 2001 Lockheed Martin received a contract for 10 LRIP F-22As, while the 2002 Defense Appropriations Act funded 13 Raptors, and requests have been made for 23 in 2003, and 27 in 2004.

F-22A Raptor
Powerplant: two Pratt & Whitney F119-PW-100 turbofans each rated at around 155.70 kN (35,000 lb st) with afterburning

Performance: max speed more than 2446 km/h (1,520 mph), initial climb rate 15240 m (50,000 ft) per min, range 3200 km (2,000 miles)

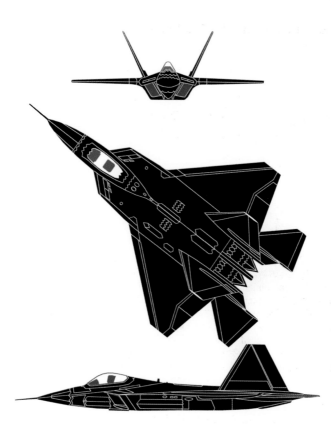

Dimensions: wing span 13.56 m (44 ft 6 in), length 18.92 m (62 ft 1 in), height 5 m (16 ft 5 in)

Recognition features
A Angular 'stealthy' shape
B Outward-canted twin fins
C Two trapezoidal engine air intakes on fuselage sides

Lockheed Martin X-35

The X-35 was Lockheed Martin's entry for the Joint Strike Fighter (JSF) competition where it was in competition with the Boeing X-32. The first X-35 prototype, in X-35A configuration, first flew on 24 October 2000. The USAF has a requirement for about 2,036 aircraft based on the standard X-35A (above) as an F-16 replacement and in this form it lands and takes off conventionally. The X-35B was a STOVL version with an additional lift fan, vectoring exhausts and lateral roll nozzles. Around 642 of the STOVL variant are required for the USMC and perhaps as many as 150 for the RAF/RN. A conventional take-off and landing 'CV variant' for the US Navy (and possibly the RN) was designated X-35C. The USN has a requirement for about 300 such machines to replace the last of its F/A-18Cs and to supplement the F/A-18E/F. The X-35C was based on the X-35A but with a larger tail and wing with tip folding for improved carrier-based operation. The X-35 was highly agile and had excellent stealth characteristics assisted by similar wing and tailplane sweep angles and by reverse-angled engine inlets. Its internal weapons bays could contain two 907-kg (2,000-lb) class air-to-ground weapons and two AAMs. On 26 October 2001 it was announced that Lockheed Martin, in partnership with BAE Systems and Northrop Grumman, had won the JSF competition and that the X-35 would be developed for service as the F-35 in A, B and C variants.

X-35B
Powerplant: one Pratt & Whitney F119 turbofan providing a maximum of 164.60 kN (37,000 lb st) for vertical lift

Performance: max speed (estimated) 1931 km/h (1,200 mph), range 3040 km (1,900 miles)

Dimensions: wing span 10.70 m (35 ft 1¼ in), length 15.47 m (50 ft 9 in), height (estimated) 5.18 m (17 ft)

Recognition features
A Angular 'stealthy' shape
B Deep forward fuselage
C Forward-swept engine air intake outer walls

McDonnell Douglas/BAe Harrier II   *USA/UK*

As a follow on to the first generation Harrier, including the RAF's Harrier GR.Mk 3 and the USMC's AV-8A and AV-8C, McDonnell Douglas and BAe developed the Harrier II. The new aircraft has a larger, carbon-fibre, wing; advanced aerodynamic devices, including LERXes; and a cockpit revised in both layout and position. The first FSD AV-8B flew for the first time on 5 November 1981 and the USMC received its initial production aircraft in 1983. All production aircraft have British-built rear fuselages. In addition, the RAF's Harrier GR.Mk 5s had many changes compared to the US aircraft, including much UK equipment. From September 1989 all USMC Harrier IIs were delivered as Night Attack aircraft with a FLIR in a fairing above the nose and other equipment. The RAF equivalent is the Harrier GR.Mk 7, to which the majority of GR.Mk 5s was converted. Both the USMC and RAF also procured two-seaters, as TAV-8Bs and T.Mk 10s respectively. Both the Italian and Spanish navies also received Harrier IIs. On 22 September 1992 the first of the USMC's Harrier II Plus (above) aircraft was flown with an APG-65 radar in the nose. Some 72 USMC aircraft were converted, while Spain and Italy both received new-build II Pluses.

AV-8B Harrier II Plus
Powerplant: one 105.87-kN (23,800-lb st) Rolls-Royce F402-RR-408 (Pegasus 11-61) vectored thrust turbofan

Performance: max speed 1065 km/h (662 mph), max climb rate at sea level 4485 m (14,715 ft) per min, service ceiling more than 15240 m (50,000 ft), combat radius 167 km (103 miles)

Dimensions: wing span 9.25 m (30 ft 4 in), length 14.12 m (46 ft 4 in), height 3.55 m (11 ft 8 in)

Recognition features
A Bicycle undercarriage with outriggers
B Anhedralled wings and tailplanes
C Raised cockpit

Mikoyan MiG-29 'Fulcrum'   *Russia*

The MiG-29 'Fulcrum' is a lightweight air defence fighter developed in the mid-1970s and the first prototype flew on 6 October 1977. Production MiG-29s entered service in 1983. The aircraft has a virtual-delta wing with large forward fairings, twin fins and prominent air intakes for the twin RD-33 turbofans. It has an all-moving tailplane and, in early models, additional ventral fins. Armament is carried on six underwing and one centreline pylons. Variants include the MiG-29A and B export models for many countries including Bulgaria, Czechoslovakia, Cuba, India, Iran, Iraq, Poland and North Korea, the MiG-29 'Fulcrum-C' and improved MiG-29S with a raised fuselage line containing additional fuel and ECM equipment, the MiG-29M with a lightened airframe and additional fuel, the MiG-29K naval variant with folding outer wings and eight wing pylons, and the MiG-29SMT which is an upgraded version with a large conformal fuel tank on the upper fuselage and RD-43 engines. An even more advanced version, based on the MiG-29K and designated MiG-29M2 or MiG-29 MRCA, was unveiled in late 2001. Tandem two-seat trainers include the MiG-29UB and the MiG-29UBT with the conformal fuel tank. Around 1,500 MiG-29s have been built by MiG-MAPO and production is now largely for export customers with around 22 non-Russian countries currently operating the aircraft.

MiG-29S 'Fulcrum-C'
Powerplant: two Klimov/Sarkisov RD-33 turbofans each rated at 81.40 kN (18,300 lb st) with afterburning

Performance: max speed 1497 km/h (930 mph), initial climb rate 11582 m (38,000 ft) per min, service ceiling 18000 m (59,060 ft), range 2100 km (1,305 miles)

Dimensions: wing span 11.35 m (37 ft 3 in), length 16.28 m (53 ft 5 in), height 4.72 m (15 ft 6 in)

Recognition features
A Large raked engine air intakes beneath wing root extensions
B Twin outwardly-canted fins
C Engine exhaust nozzles toed outwards

McDonnell Douglas F-4 Phantom II   *USA*

The superb Phantom II first flew on 27 May 1958, with the USN designation YF4H-1. Normally, the F-4 is fitted with two General Electric J79 turbojets, variants remaining in service including the F-4D, multirole F-4E with a 20-mm six-barrelled nose cannon, the Luftwaffe's F-4F (right), Japan's F-4EJ Kai, and the recce RF-4C and RF-4E. Many redundant F-4 airframes have been converted as target drones for the US military.

Recognition features A Low wing with dihedralled outer panels **B** Sharply anhedralled tailplanes **C** Broad-chord fin

Mikoyan-Gurevich MiG-23 'Flogger'   *USSR*

The MiG-23 first flew on 10 June 1967 with first deliveries being made to Soviet forces in 1973. The MiG-23 'Flogger' variants include the initial MiG-23S, the main-production MiG-23M (right), the MiG-23ML and MiG-23P with increased power and lighter gross weight, the MiG-23MLD, and the MiG-23B (and BK, BM and BN) fighter-bomber with a slim pointed nose. The MiG-27 is similar to the MiG-23BM but has fixed air intakes and a modified afterburner. A tandem two-seat MiG-23UB was also built.

Recognition features A Shoulder-mounted VG wing **B** Huge fin fillet **C** Folding ventral fin

Mitsubishi F-2   *Japan*

The F-2 is based on the F-16C and was developed jointly by Mitsubishi and Lockheed Martin. The prototype single-seat XF-2A (right) first flew on 7 October 1995 and a further XF-2A and two XF-2B two-seaters have been used in the development programme. Changes from the F-16C include an enlarged composite wing, a new cockpit canopy with a separate windshield, modified wing leading edge root extensions and a revised under-fuselage profile to accommodate the General Electric F110-GE-129 reheated turbofan. Production deliveries were initiated in late 1999 to meet a revised JASDF requirement for 130 F-2s.

Recognition features A Very similar to F-16 **B** Forward swept trailing edge on large-area wing **C** Revised tailplane shape and deeper ventral fins

Mikoyan MiG-AT

Russia

The MiG-AT is a private-venture advanced jet trainer with combat capability, developed by MiG-MAPO to a Russian air force requirement. It is in competition with the Yakovlev/Aermacchi Yak-130. The MiG-AT is a low-wing tandem two-seater with two SNECMA Larzac turbofans fitted above the inner wing sections and it has fly-by-wire systems and French Sextant avionics. During development the engine nacelles were lengthened, with the engine air intakes being moved to a point ahead of the wing. The prototype first flew on 16 March 1996 and two development aircraft were built, the second having underwing pylons. Up to seven hardpoints are available on the proposed MiG-AS single-seat light fighter. MiG-MAPO also has plans for a MiG-UTS for Russia; MiG-ATS combat trainer; MiG-AP MP aircraft; and MiG-ATK naval trainer with arrester gear, folding wings and French avionics; MiG-ATSK naval combat trainer and MiG-ASK naval single seater. By late 1999 only a small evaluation batch had been ordered by the Russian air force, and the first production aircraft was rolled out on 7 June 2001.

MiG-AT
Powerplant: two 14.20-kN (3,175 lb st) SNECMA Larzac 04-R20 turbofans

Performance: max speed 853 km/h (530 mph), cruising speed 772 km/h (480 mph), initial climb rate 3962 m (13,000 ft) per min, service ceiling 15500 m (50,860 ft), range 2576 km (1,610 miles)

Dimensions: wing span 10.16 m (33 ft 4 in), length 12.01 m (39 ft 5 in), height 4.62 m (15 ft 2 in)

Recognition features
A Low-set wing with engine intakes above root
B Tall fin with mid-set tailplane
C Straight wing with exhaust nozzles aft of trailing edge

Mikoyan-Gurevich MiG-21 'Fishbed'   *USSR*

The MiG-21 'Fishbed' has a highly swept delta wing, a conventional fin and tailplane and a retractable tricycle undercarriage with the main wing-mounted units folding inwards. The cockpit is faired into the fuselage with a spine which runs back to the fin leading edge. The prototype first flew on 16 June 1955 and the first large-scale production aircraft was the MiG-21F-13 'Fishbed-C'. Later variants included the MiG-21P with an enlarged spine fairing, MiG-21PF (and export MiG-21FL) with a broader vertical tail, ventral gun pack and modified radar, and the MiG-21PFS and MiG-21PFM with a separate windshield and canopy and more power. The MiG-21PFM was employed in several versions including the MiG-21R tactical recce model, and the related MiG-21S and MiG-21SM (export MiG-21M) were air superiority fighters. The final MiG-21 derivative was the MiG-21bis with a much-enlarged dorsal spine. In addition to the single-seat MiG-21s, the tandem two-seat MiG-21U and MiG-21UM 'Mongol' trainers were built. Major upgrades are being carried out by Hindustan in conjunction with MiG-MAPO (MiG-21-93 or MiG-21I) and by Aerostar in Romania with Elbit (Lancer, above). The Chengdu J-7 (F-7 for export) first flew on 17 January 1966 and is similar to the MiG-21F-13. The F-7M Airguard is an air defence variant. The Guizhou JJ-7 (export FT-7) is a two-seat trainer model.

MiG-21MF 'Fishbed-J'
Powerplant: one Tumanski R-13-300 turbojet rated at 63.66 kN (14,307 lb st) with afterburning

Performance: max speed 2180 km/h (1,355 mph), initial climb rate 9144 m (30,000 ft) per min, range 1792 km (1,120 miles)

Dimensions: wing span 7.14 m (23 ft 5 in), length 12.29 m (40 ft 4 in), height 4.50 m (14 ft 9 in)

Recognition features
A Short-span delta wing
B Pitot engine air intake with conical centrebody
C Pitot tube mounted above intake

Mikoyan-Gurevich MiG-25 & MiG-31 *Russia*

The MiG-25 'Foxbat' was developed in the late 1950s as a high-altitude fighter to intercept new-generation American high-performance recce aircraft and strategic bombers such as the B-70 Valkyrie. First flown on 6 March 1964 as the Ye-155R, it is a very large Mach-3 aircraft built around two reheated Tumanski turbofans. It has a shoulder-mounted wing, twin vertical fins and a low-set tailplane. The retractable tricycle undercarriage has large single main wheels and the MiG-25 is fitted with four underwing missile pylons. Variants included the initial MiG-25P which went into service in 1973, the MiG-25PU (above) trainer with an additional cockpit and no radar, the MiG-25PD with improved engines and modified radar and MiG-25PDS with an extended nose, the MiG-25R recce aircraft and the MiG-25RB bomber. The MiG-31 'Foxhound', which first flew as the MiG-25MP on 16 September 1975, is a substantially redesigned MiG-25 with a larger fuselage, wing leading edge extensions, a tandem two-seat cockpit and twin-wheel main under-carriage units. Offensive weapons are carried on wing and fuselage pylons and the aircraft has a 'Flashdance' fire-control radar, and the MiG-31 and improved MiG-31M are powered by two 151.95-kN (34,170-lb st) Soloviev D-30F6 reheated turbofans. Nearly 1,200 MiG-25s were built, a number being exported. Around 400 MiG-31s are believed to have been completed but none has been exported.

MiG-25RB 'Foxbat-B'
Powerplant: two Tumanski R-15BD-300 turbofans each rated at 109.83 kN (24,691 lb st) with afterburning

Performance: max speed 3001 km/h (1,865 mph), initial climb rate 13533 m (44,400 ft) per min, service ceiling 21000 m (68,900 ft), range 2088 km (1,305 miles)

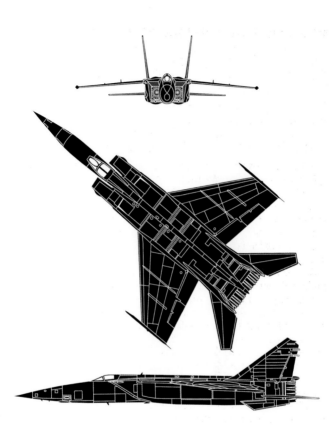

Dimensions: wing span 13.39 m (43 ft 11 in), length 21.56 m (70 ft 9 in), height 5.99 m (19 ft 8 in)

Recognition features
A Sharply raked, large rectangular engine air intakes
B Twin outwardly canted fins
C Rectangular section, boxy fuselage

Nanchang K-8 Karakorum 8 *China/Pakistan*

The K-8 is a two-seat primary jet trainer jointly developed by the Nanchang Aircraft Factory and the Pakistan Military Aeronautical Complex. The K-8 (above), which made its first flight on 21 November 1990, has a straight low-set wing, air intakes on the fuselage sides and a retractable tricycle undercarriage. The tandem cockpit is enclosed by a sideways-opening canopy and the aircraft has four underwing hard-points for weapons training stores and a centreline strongpoint for a 23-mm cannon pod. An initial batch of six K-8s has been delivered to the Pakistan air force, powered by the Honeywell TFE731 turbofan, 12 went to Myanmar and 8 are on order for Sri Lanka. The K-8 as required by the air force of the People's Republic of China is to be powered by a Progress ZMKB AI-25-TL turbofan and designated K-8J, and around 30 of this variant have been delivered. Export customers also include Egypt which ordered 80 K-8Es with TFE731 engines, the first of which flew on 5 July 2000; Namibia which received four K-8s in 1999 and Zambia, which received eight aircraft in 1999. Zambia is reported to have eight further options for the type and interest has been expressed by many more potential customers. An experimental variable-stability prototype is designated K-8SVA.

K-8 Karakorum 8
Powerplant: one 16.01-kN
(3,600-lb st) Honeywell
TFE731-2A turbofan

Performance: max speed
805 km/h (500 mph), cruising
speed 740 km/h (460 mph), take-
off run 440 m (1,445 ft), initial
climb rate 1622 m (5,320 ft) per
min, range 2237 km (1,398 miles)

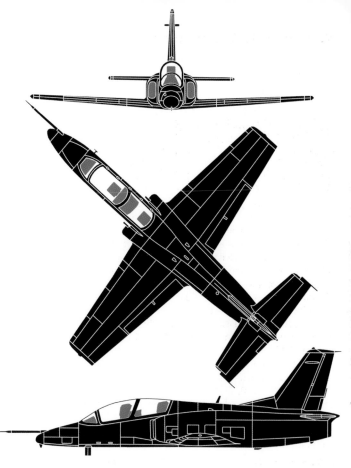

Dimensions: wing span 9.63 m (31 ft 7 in), length 11.58 m (38 ft), height 4.22 m (13 ft 10 in)

Recognition features
A Low-set straight wing
B Pitot mounted above nose cone
C Single engine exhaust nozzle in rear fuselage

Mil Mi-8 and Mi-17 'Hip' *Russia*

The Mi-8 'Hip' prototype, designated V-8, first flew in 1961. The 'Hip' is powered by two Isotov TV2 turboshafts. Military variants include the Mi-8T, armed Mi-8TB, Mi-8MB aeromedical version and Mi-9 airborne command helicopter. The Mi-17 is an improved Mi-8. Its main military versions are the Mi-17MT (Russian service designation Mi-8M), Mi-17P for communications jamming with a large rear fuselage antenna array, export Mi-17M, Mi-17MD (right) transport with a rear ramp in place of the clamshell doors and an enlarged radar nose, and the stretched Mi-173 (formerly Mi-18) with retractable U/C.

Recognition features A Large fuel tanks on lower fuselage sides
B Round cabin windows **C** Mi-17 tail rotor on port side

Mil Mi-24 'Hind' *Russia*

The Mi-24 'Hind' is unique in combining full anti-tank capability with an eight-troop cabin. The engines and dynamic systems were largely taken from the Mi-8. Early Mi-24s had a large 'glasshouse' cockpit with a 12.7-mm (0.5-in) machine-gun in the nose, but the later Mi-24D has bubble cockpits and a chin-mounted turret. The Mi-24V is an upgraded version with improved systems. Alternative weapons are used in the Mi-24P (right) and Mi-24VP, and the Mi-24K is for army recce, while the Mi-24PS is for police support operations. The Mi-25 and Mi-35 are export versions.

Recognition features A Stepped tandem cockpits **B** Cabin
C Anhedralled stub wings

Mil Mi-28 'Havoc' *Russia*

The Mi-28 'Havoc' was designed to a Russian army requirement, but lost to the Ka-50. Nevertheless, the Mi-28 is being offered for export. It is conventional in external layout and has two Isotov TV3-117 turboshafts in separate pods either side of the main rotor pylon. The Mi-28 has stub wings with two weapons pylons and tip mountings for countermeasures pods. A turret beneath the nose houses a 30-mm cannon. The prototype Mi-28A first flew on 10 November 1982. The Mi-28N night-attack version (right) first flew on 14 November 1996.

Recognition features A Stepped tandem cockpits with small, angular glazed panels **B** N has ball turret on rotor mast

Northrop F-5 Tiger II

The F-5 Tiger II was developed from the original F-5 Freedom Fighter. Externally, the F-5 closely resembles the T-38 Talon advanced trainer but it is a single-seater with a much stronger airframe and more powerful J85-GE-13 turbojets. The wing was redesigned incorporating leading edge extensions and a multi-spar design in place of the T-38's honeycomb structure so that four underwing hardpoints and wingtip Sidewinder rails could be accommodated. Northrop flew the prototype on 30 July 1959 and this was followed by the definitive F-5A and, on 24 February 1964, by the first F-5B tandem two-seat combat-capable conversion trainer. Some were built or converted as tactical recce RF-5As. The F-5E Tiger II (above) (and two-seat F-5F) is an improved version which first flew on 11 August 1972 and has more power, increased weapons load and modified systems. Initial F-5 deliveries went to the USAF but the F-5A/F-5B and later F-5E were also supplied to 27 other countries including Brazil, Greece, the Philippines, Saudi Arabia, Turkey, Venezuela and Switzerland. Licence assembly took place in Switzerland, Taiwan, South Korea and by Canadair for the CAF (CF-5A/CF-5D or CF-116) and by CASA for the Spanish air force (C.9/CE.9). Many upgrades have been carried out including the Chilean F-5 Plus Tiger III with an advanced cockpit system. In total 2,084 single-seat and 534 two-seat F-5s had been built when production ceased in 1987.

F-5E Tiger II

Powerplant: two General Electric J85-GE-21B turbojets each rated at 22.20 kN (5,000 lb st) with afterburning

Performance: max speed 1698 km/h (1,055 mph), initial climb rate 10363 m (34,000 ft) per min, service ceiling 15590 m (51,800 ft), range 3696 km (2,310 miles)

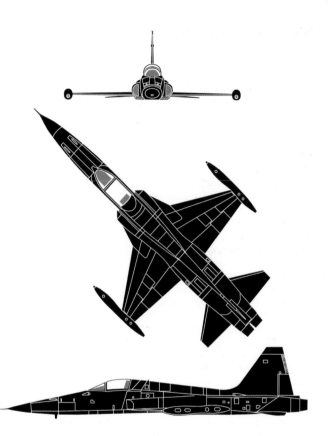

Dimensions: wing span 8.13 m (26 ft 8 in), length 14.45 m (47 ft 5 in), height 4.09 m (13 ft 5 in)

Recognition features
A Low-set, short-span straight wings
B Prominent LERXes
C Long, oval-section forward fuselage

Northrop Grumman B-2 Spirit

USA

Drawing on its extensive experience of large flying wing aircraft gleaned during the early post-war years, Northrop developed the B-2 as a fully 'stealthy' strategic bomber to replace the increasingly aged B-52. The B-2 first flew on 17 July 1990. It has a highly swept wing with a unique jagged edge profile to the rear wing and fuselage, a blended body containing the two-crew flight deck and two large weapons bays in the central belly. The retractable tricycle undercarriage has two four-wheel main bogies and a twin nosewheel unit. The B-2 relies on a radar-absorbing structure of epoxy-graphite honeycomb for its stealth characteristics but, as in the F-117A, several straight surfaces are broken into jagged shapes to reduce the radar signature. The operational B-2A Spirit also employs anti-radar surface finishes and various classified systems are also said to be in use. The weapons load of the B-2 can be up to 16 AGM-129 cruise missiles, while up to 34019 kg (75,000 lb) of conventional bombs can be carried as an alternative. Some 21 B-2As have been delivered to date but further procurement relies on funding approval. The type has seen combat over the Balkans and Afghanistan.

B-2A Spirit
Powerplant: four 84.52-kN
(19,000-lb st) General Electric
F118-GE-110 turbofans

Performance: max speed
982 km/h (610 mph), cruising
speed 954 km/h (593 mph), initial
climb rate 914 m (3,000 ft) per
min, range 18400 km
(11,500 miles)

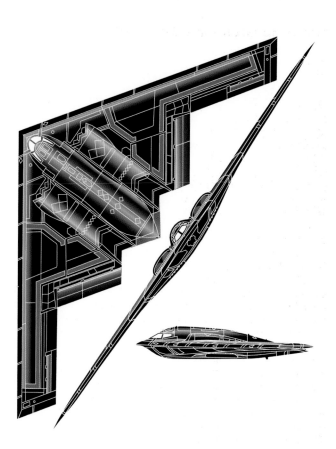

Dimensions: wing span 52.42 m (172 ft), length 21.03 m (69 ft), height 5.18 m (17 ft)

Recognition features
A Unique configuration
B No vertical tail surfaces
C Flying wing with central fuselage nacelle

Northrop Grumman E-2 Hawkeye USA

Grumman designed the Hawkeye to replace the smaller E-1B Tracer carrier-based airborne radar picket which was itself a development of the C-1A Trader. The Hawkeye first flew on 21 October 1960 and production is expected to continue until at least 2007. It is a high-wing aircraft with a four-fin tail unit, retractable tricycle undercarriage and two wing-mounted Rolls-Royce T56 turboprops. The circular-section fuselage houses two flight crew and five operators for the long-range radar which is contained in a 7.32-m (24-ft) diameter rotating radome on a strutted rear fuselage pylon. Deliveries of the E-2A (formerly W2F-1) started in January 1964 and most E-2As were subsequently upgraded to E-2B standard with an improved Litton L-304 computer and larger outer tail fins. The E-2C (above), which is now the standard service version, had a new AN/APS-111 radar and later upgrades and new-production aircraft incorporated the APS-138 and APS-145. The E-2C has been exported to Egypt, France, Israel, Japan, Singapore and Taiwan and total Hawkeye production exceeds 250 aircraft. The latest Hawkeye 2000 has upgraded computers and workstations and improved satcom equipment, allowing it to link with other airborne sensors, and is being built for the US Navy, France and Taiwan.

E-2C Hawkeye
Powerplant: two 3803-kW (5,100-shp) Rolls-Royce T56-A-427 turboprops

Performance: max speed 628 km/h (390 mph), cruising speed 602 km/h (374 mph), initial climb rate 884 m (2,900 ft) per min, service ceiling 11275 m (37,000 ft), range 2832 km (1,770 miles)

Dimensions: wing span 24.56 m (80 ft 7 in), length 17.60 m (57 ft 9 in), height 5.59 m (18 ft 4 in)

Recognition features
A Rear-fuselage mounted rotodome
B Twin turboprops in deep nacelles
C Four vertical tail surfaces

Northrop Grumman E-8 J-STARS   *USA*

The E-8 J-STARS (Joint Surveillance Target Attack System) was developed initially by Grumman, and later Northrop Grumman, to fulfill much the same role in the ground war that AWACS plays in the air. The basic Boeing 707-300 airframe was chosen as the platform for the AN/APY-3 multi-mode SLAR that is at the heart of the E-8's systems. This radar has its antenna located in a long 'canoe' radome under the forward fuselage. The first two E-8s made the system's combat debut during Operation *Desert Storm* in 1991, even before it was fully operational. The type's stunning performance during that conflict ensured its future with the USAF and the operational E-8C (above) is in line for upgrades which may include more economical CFM56 turbofans, as well as a new radar system, which is due to be in service by 2006. The US government continues to fund J-STARS acquisition, with the USAF having stated a total requirement for 19 machines. In the light of the shortfall in US surveillance systems that has been revealed over Afghanistan, the procurement and enhancement of the E-8 is likely to gain in importance.

E-8C J-STARS
Powerplant: four 85.40-kN (19,200-lb st) Pratt & Whitney TF33-P-102C turbofans

Performance: max operating speed 892 km/h (555 mph), service ceiling 12800 m (42,000 ft), maximum endurance on internal fuel 11 hours, maximum endurance with one inflight refuelling 20 hours

Dimensions: wing span 44.42 m
(145 ft 9 in), length 46.61 m
(152 ft 11 in), height 12.95 m
(42 ft 6 in)

Recognition features
A Large canoe fairing beneath
forward fuselage
B Low, swept wing
C Four turbofan engines

Panavia Tornado

International

The Tornado is standard equipment with the air arms of Britain, Germany (air force and navy), Italy and Saudi Arabia and distinguished itself in the Gulf War and over the Balkans. The Tornado prototype was first flown on 14 August 1974 and was built by the Panavia consortium of DASA, Alenia and BAe. Tornado is a tandem two-seater with VG wings which carry weapons on four automatically aligning pylons. A further three fuselage hardpoints are available and the Tornado IDS (Interdictor/Strike) has two fixed 27-mm IWKA-Mauser cannon in the nose. Variants include the standard Tornado IDS (RAF GR.Mk 1), the dual-control combat-capable GR.Mk 1(T), the recce Tornado GR.Mk 1A and anti-shipping GR.Mk 1B. Germany and Italy fly recce/SEAD Tornado ECR (Electronic Combat and Reconnaissance) aircraft. The GR.Mk 4 (above) (and GR.Mk 4A) are RAF mid-life upgrades with much extra equipment. The Tornado ADV is the dedicated long-range air defence variant, first flown on 27 October 1979. Originally delivered to the RAF as the Tornado F.Mk 2, it differs from the IDS in having a longer fuselage, a new long-range Marconi intercept radar, a retractable refuelling probe, a single cannon and four belly-mounted Sky Flash AAMs. The later F.Mk 3 has a modified afterburner. The Tornado ADV is also flown by Italy and Saudi Arabia.

Tornado GR.Mk 4
Powerplant: two Turbo Union RB199 Mk 103 turbofans each rated at 71.20 kN (16,000 lb st) with afterburning

Performance: max speed 1481 km/h (921 mph), initial climb rate (estimated) 13716 m (45,000 ft) per min, service ceiling more than 15240 m (50,000 ft), range 1120 km (700 miles)

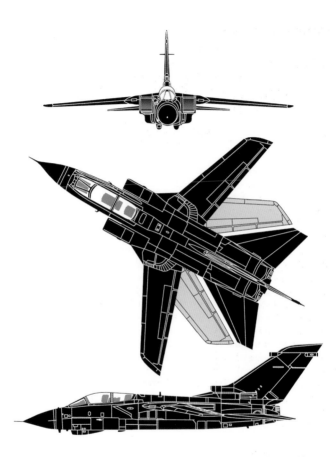

Dimensions: wing span (spread) 13.89 m (45 ft 7 in), length 16.71 m (54 ft 10 in), height 5.94 m (19 ft 6 in)

Recognition features
A Tall, broad-chord fin
B High-set swing wings
C Sharply raked, rectangular-section engine air intakes

NH Industries NH 90 *International*

The NH 90 has been developed by the NH Industries consortium set up in 1985 by Aérospatiale, MBB, Agusta and Fokker. It is largely built from composites, has four-bladed rotors, and its twin RTM322 turboshafts located on top of the fuselage. The Italian version will have GE/Alfa Romeo T700-T6E engines. The two main versions are the NFH 90 (naval frigate-based SAR and ASW) and TTH 90 (army tactical transport with provision for external weapons). The first of five flying prototypes flew on 18 December 1995. Funding delays meant that no deliveries had been made by the end of 2001 but orders have been placed by Finland, France, Germany, Italy, the Netherlands, Norway and Sweden.

Recognition features A Angular fuselage shape **B** Retractable tricycle undercarriage **C** Low-set tailplane to starboard

Northrop T-38 Talon *USA*

Now in service for nearly 40 years, the T-38 advanced jet trainer is used in large numbers by Germany, South Korea, Turkey and the US. It was first flown as the YT-38 on 10 April 1959. The Talon is a supersonic tandem two-seat aircraft with an elegant area-ruled fuselage incorporating twin GE J85 turbojets. It has straight tapered wings and a low-set all-moving tailplane. The T-38B is a LIFT version fitted with a fuselage centreline weapons hardpoint for practice bombs or a Minigun pod.

Recognition features A Long, area-ruled fuselage **B** Flat underfuselage **C** Small engine intakes above and ahead of wing

Northrop Grumman EA-6B Prowler *USA*

Grumman's A-6A Intruder entered USN service in 1964 and during combat over Vietnam, it was supported by a handful of EA-6As converted for ECM tasks with a large fin-tip antenna housing. The EA-6B Prowler is a four-seat development of the EA-6A with a lengthened forward fuselage housing two rear seats for ECM operators and equipped with new tactical jamming systems including up to five ALQ-99 pods. The Prowler can carry offensive loads including HARMs. The EA-6B continues to be upgraded for US Navy service until at least 2015.

Recognition features A Large fin-tip 'football' fairing **B** Extensive cockpit glazing **C** Fixed refuelling probe ahead of cockpit

Pilatus PC-7 and PC-9 *Switzerland*

The PC-7 (above) basic and advanced trainer is a much improved version of the Pilatus P-3 and the prototype, which was converted from a P-3 and initially designated P-3B, was first flown on 12 April 1966. The most significant changes were the PT6A-25 turboprop engine, the modified tandem-seat cockpit with a large blister canopy and the enlarged vertical and horizontal tail surfaces. The PC-7 Turbo Trainer has six underwing hardpoints including two wet stations for fuel tanks. Around 450 PC-7s have been built, mostly for military users such as Austria, Bolivia, Chile, France, Myanmar and Uruguay, but also for some private purchasers such as the 'Patrouille Adecco' aerobatic team in France. The PC-7 Mk II M is the current version with a raised rear cockpit, glass cockpits, enlarged fin and PT6A-25C engine. Also in production in 2002 is the PC-9, which is a substantially redesigned PC-7 with a raised rear cockpit and redesigned canopy, Martin Baker Mk 11A ejection seats, a redesigned wing and an 857-kW (1,150-shp) PT6A-62 turboprop in a new cowling. Around 59 PC-9/As have been built by Hawker de Havilland in Australia and other PC-9s serve in Croatia, Iraq, Myanmar, Saudi Arabia and Slovenia. The PC-9B is a civil version adapted for target towing. A modified PC-9 is being built for the USAF by Raytheon as the T-6A Texan II.

PC-7 Mk II M Turbo Trainer
Powerplant: one 522-kW (700-shp) Pratt & Whitney Canada PT6A-25C turboprop

Performance: max speed 555 km/h (345 mph), max cruising speed 467 km/h (290 mph), initial climb rate 1170 m (2,840 ft) per min, range 1408 km (880 miles)

Dimensions: wing span 10.13 m (33 ft 3 in), length 10.13 m (33 ft 3 in), height 3.28 m (10 ft 9 in)

Recognition features
A Low-set wing
B Large fin fillet
C Original PC-7s have three-bladed propeller

Raytheon (Beech) U-21, VC-6B & C-12 *USA*

While Beech was developing the King Air it also produced a turboprop military version of the unpressurised Queen Air 80 which went into production in 1964 as the U-21A Ute (Model 65-A90-1). Used widely in Vietnam, the U-21 was modified for many roles including electronic surveillance (RU-21A, RU-21B, RU-21D, RU-21H, etc) frequently without cabin windows and with large wing-mounted blade antennae. Some standard pressurised King Air 90s were also acquired by the USAF as the VC-6B and 61 of a trainer version, the T-44A (Model H90), went to the US Navy. The Model 200 Super King Air was acquired by all four US services, over 350 having been delivered to date including the US Army C-12C and USN/Marines UC-12B with PT6A-41 engines. Many electronic monitoring and special missions variants (RC-12D, RC-12K, RC-12N (above)) were delivered to the US Army fitted with different versions of the Guardrail Comint/Elint sensor systems. The US Army also received the C-12D transport. The USAF has taken C-12A and C-12F aircraft for light transport and communications work and these, along with their US Army and Navy equivalents, serve at US bases around the world. All King Air-based C-12s are named Huron in US service. Twelve USAF Raytheon 1900s are designated C-12J.

RC-12D Guardrail V
Powerplant: two 634-kW (850-shp) Pratt & Whitney Canada PT6A-41 turboprops

Performance: max speed 480 km/h (299 mph), cruising speed 438 km/h (270 mph), initial climb rate 732 m (2,400 ft) per min, service ceiling 9420 m (30,900 ft), range 2915 km (1,822 miles)

Dimensions: wing span 17.63 m (57 ft 10 in), length 13.36 m (43 ft 10 in), height 4.57 m (15 ft)

Recognition features
A Low-set wing
B Swept T-tail
C RC-12 has massive antenna 'farms' around airframe
D Twin turboprops

Raytheon T-6 Texan II   *Switzerland/USA*

Raytheon has developed a new version of the PC-9 turboprop trainer for use by the USAF and USN. This won the 1995 JPATS competition and over 700 are expected to be delivered as the T-6A Texan II. Initially named Beech Mk II (above, foreground), the first Beech-built production prototype (Model PD.373) first flew in December 1992. The aircraft has been extensively modified with a strengthened airframe and a PT6A-68 turboprop, and it has a three-piece canopy, modified tailplane and increased fuel capacity. The first production aircraft flew in July 1998 and the Texan went into USAF service in mid-1999. It has also been ordered by Chile and Greece, while 24 aircraft for use by the Canadian Armed Forces in the NATO Flying Training in Canada scheme have been ordered as Harvard IIs.

T-6A Texan II
Powerplant: one 1268-kW (1,700-shp) Pratt & Whitney Canada PT6A-68 turboprop

Performance: max speed 574 km/h (357 mph), max cruising speed 426 km/h (265 mph), initial climb rate 958 m (3,145 ft) per min, range 1656 km (1,036 miles)

Dimensions: wing span 10.19 m (33 ft 5 in), length 10.17 m (33 ft 4 in), height 3.26 m (10 ft 8 in)

Recognition features

A Long, tapered forward fuselage

B Ventral fins on rear fuselage

C Wing planform revised compared to PC-9

Rockwell B-1B Lancer   *USA*

Rockwell originally designed the supersonic B-1A nuclear bomber to meet the USAF's Advanced Manned Strategic Aircraft Requirement. The B-1A, which first flew on 23 December 1974, had a streamlined fuselage with a cruciform tail and a forward four-person crew compartment. In 1977 the programme was cancelled by the Carter administration however, before re-emerging in 1981 as the less-complex and less-highly performing B-1B. The B-1B has VG wings and less-complex engine air intakes than the highly-supersonic B-1A. The definitive production B-1B Lancer, which commenced deliveries in 1985, has had its weapons capability steadily evolved in a series of ongoing upgrades. Basically, it has three separate bomb bays in the fuselage for a maximum load of 34019 kg (75,000 lb) and it can carry either conventional free-fall nuclear weapons, up to 84 standard Mk 82 HE bombs or a variety of guided weapons including the AGM-86 air-launched cruise missile. Rockwell built four B-1A development aircraft and delivered the last of 100 B-1Bs in January 1988. The majority of these continues in USAF service, despite a series of operational and political problems which have affected the aircraft. The B-1B made its combat debut during Operation *Desert Fox* in 1998 and has fought over the Balkans and Afghanistan.

B-1B Lancer
Powerplant: four General Electric F101-GE-102 turbofans each rated at 136.90 kN (30,780 lb st) with afterburning

Performance: max speed 1328 km/h (825 mph), penetration speed at 61 m (200 ft) more than 965 km/h (600 mph), range 11928 km (7,455 miles)

Dimensions: wing span (spread) 41.67 m (136 ft 8½ in), length 44.80 m (147 ft), height 10.62 m (34 ft 10 in)

Recognition features
A Low-set swept wing
B Four engines housed in pairs either side of the rear fuselage
C Long forward fuselage with bulged cockpit area

PZL Swidnik W-3 Sokól   *Poland*

With experience of building large numbers of Mi-2s and Kanias, PZL Swidnik developed the medium-capacity W-3 Sokól, flying the prototype on 16 November 1979. The Sokól's tail boom mounts a three-bladed tail rotor and it has a fixed tricycle undercarriage. The twin PZL-10W turboshafts drive a four-bladed composite main rotor. The Sokól can be fitted with outrigger weapons hardpoints. Variants include the W-3A (right), armed W-3W, the W-3RM Anakonda SAR helicopter and the S-1W Huzar anti-tank version. The Sokól flies with the Czech Republic, the German Border Police, Myanmar and Poland.

Recognition features A Pointed nose **B** Engines in prominent nacelles below main rotor **C** Long tail boom compared to cabin

Rockwell T-2 Buckeye   *USA*

The Buckeye is an advanced jet trainer designed for the USN for carrier deck landing training and weapons instruction. It has a raised cruciform tail and the first YT2J-1 was first flown on 31 January 1958, with a single Westinghouse J34-WE-36 turbojet. As the T2J-1 Buckeye (later T-2A) it entered service in mid-1959. The in-service T-2C has two 13.10-kN (2,950 lb st) GE J85-GE-4 turbojets mounted side by side, additional fuel and a taller undercarriage. The export T-2D was sold to Venezuela, and the T-2E (right) to Greece.

Recognition features A Stepped tandem cockpit **B** Engine air intakes low down on forward fuselage **C** Mid-set straight wing with tip tanks

SIAI-Marchetti S.211   *Italy*

First flown on 10 April 1981, the S.211 is a tandem two-seat jet trainer tailored to the needs of emergent air arms. It was intended for low-cost basic instruction, with the flexibility of four wing pylons to facilitate tactical weapons training. Alternatively it could be used as a light-attack aircraft. The S.211 has a Pratt & Whitney JT15D turbofan and was bought by Haiti, the Philippines and Singapore. In 1991 Agusta (which had acquired SIAI) teamed with Grumman to unsuccessfully offer the S.211A in the JPATS competition. All rights to the S.211 now rest with Aermacchi. **Recognition features A** Stepped tandem cockpit **B** Mid-set, moderately swept wing **C** Tailcone fairing

Saab 37 Viggen   *Sweden*

The Viggen is the Swedish Air Force's second-generation supersonic interceptor, developed by Saab during the early 1960s. Its innovative design, aimed at achieving maximum agility and STOL performance, incorporated a complex delta wing positioned at the rear of the fuselage and a large fully-moving canard surface forward. It is powered by a reheated RM8 (Pratt & Whitney JT8D-22) engine equipped with a thrust reversal system. Saab first flew the prototype on 8 February 1967 and the Swedish Air Force eventually acquired 329 aircraft. The initial AJ 37 attack variant is able to carry a mixture of ASMs, AAMs and anti-ship missiles. The JA 37 (above) is an interceptor version with improved look down/shoot down radar, a higher-thrust engine, a slightly longer fuselage and an integral 30-mm cannon, and the SF 37 has photo-reconnaissance capability with a camera nose and the ability to carry external ECM and sensor pods. The SH 37 was designed for all-weather MR and maritime attack. Some 98 Viggens were updated to AJS 37 standard with advanced datalinks and improved radar surveillance systems, AJSF 37 and AJSH 37 standards and the JA 37 is now capable of carrying AMRAAMs. No export sales of the Viggen were made, and the type is very much in the twilight of its Swedish Air Force career.

JA 37 Viggen
Powerplant: one Volvo Flygmotor RM8B turbofan rated at 125.05 kN (28,110 lb st) with afterburning

Performance: max speed 2125 km/h (1,320 mph), initial climb rate 6025 m (19,767 ft) per min, take-off run about 400 m (1,312 ft), range 2000 km (1,250 miles)

Dimensions: wing span 10.59 m (34 ft 9 in), length 16.41 m (53 ft 10 in), height 5.89 m (19 ft 4 in)

Recognition features
A Canards mounted high on intake trunks
B Engine exhaust nozzle within rear fuselage
C Delta wing

Saab JAS 39 Gripen   *Sweden*

The need to replace the Viggen resulted in Saab designing a completely new multi-role combat aircraft which would have enhanced capability, but would be less costly to acquire and operate. The JAS 39 Gripen continues with Saab's delta wing layout and has forward canard control surfaces, but it is less than half the weight of the Viggen and is built with a significant proportion of composites. With an internal 27-mm cannon and six hardpoints, it can carry a similar offensive load to that of the Viggen and is fitted with the latest technology cockpit systems including a HUD and a three-screen glass cockpit. The Gripen prototype, powered by a licence-built General Electric F404J turbofan, was first flown on 9 December 1988 and variants include the JAS 39A multi-role single-seater and the stretched JAS 39B (above) tandem two-seat combat-capable trainer. The JAS 39C, which is the basis for the export version being produced in cooperation with BAE Systems, is under development, powered by a Volvo Flygmotor RM12 Plus engine. First Swedish air force deliveries were made in June 1996 and an order subsequently came from South Africa, while the Czech Republic and Hungary both look set to lease the type.

JAS 39A Gripen
Powerplant: one Volvo Flygmotor RM12 turbofan rated at 80.54 kN (18,105 lb st) with afterburning

Performance: max speed more than 1223 km/h (760 mph), take-off run 800 m (2,625 ft), combat radius about 800 km (497 miles)

Dimensions: wing span 8.41 m (27 ft 7 in), length 14.10 m (46 ft 3 in), height 4.50 m (14 ft 9 in)

Recognition features
A Sharply-swept canards on intake trunks
B Delta wing with no tailplanes
C Large conical nose radome

SEPECAT Jaguar   *France/UK*

The Jaguar ground attack aircraft has distinguished itself in European and Middle Eastern conflicts and remains in front-line service. It is the result of cooperation between British Aircraft Corporation (later BAe) and Breguet (later Dassault-Breguet) as SEPECAT (Société Européenne de Production de l'Avion de l'Ecole de Combat et d'Appui Tactique). The Jaguar has a compound-sweep wing, ahead of which are intakes for its reheated turbofans. It has four underwing hardpoints, two overwing pylons for AAMs and a centreline position. The prototype Jaguar first flew on 8 September 1968. Both single-seat and tandem two-seat combat-capable trainer versions were built as the Jaguar S (GR.Mk 1 and later GR.Mk 1A (above)) and Jaguar B (T.Mk 2) respectively, for the RAF and Jaguar A and Jaguar E for l'Armée de l'Air. Jaguar International is the export version, 42 of which were sold in single- and two-seat forms and delivered to Oman (Jaguar OS and two-seat OB), Nigeria (Jaguar SN and two-seat BN) and Ecuador (Jaguar ES and two-seat EB). For the Indian Air Force the Jaguar was manufactured by Hindustan Aircraft, which continues to build the single-seat Jaguar IS and two-seat Jaguar IT, and which delivered the last of 10 single-seat Jaguar IM anti-shipping aircraft with conical nose radomes in 1999. The Jaguar has been massively updated in RAF service to GR.Mk 3A and T.Mk 4 standards for precision attack with TIALD and laser-guided munitions.

Jaguar GR.Mk 1
Powerplant: two Rolls-Royce/Turboméca Adour Mk 104 turbofans each rated at 35.75 kN (8,040 lb st) with afterburning

Performance: max speed 1698 km/h (1,055 mph), initial climb rate 6096 m (20,000 ft) per min, range 1696 km (1,060 miles)

Dimensions: wing span 8.69 m (28 ft 6 in), length 16.84 m (55 ft 3 in), height 4.90 m (16 ft 1 in)

Recognition features
A High-set wing
B Square-section engine air intakes with large auxiliary doors
C Stalky, undercarriage located in fuselage

Shenyang J-8/F-8IIM

China

Following a long period of manufacture of the MiG-21 (J-7), Chinese designers developed the J-8 high-altitude Mach 2.2 air superiority fighter in the mid-1960s. The prototype J-8 was completed and flown for the first time by the Shenyang factory on 5 July 1969. Broadly based on the J-7, the J-8 was a larger aircraft with two 59.81-kN (13,450 lb st) Guizhou WP-7B reheated turbojets positioned side by side in the rear fuselage. It retained the nose air intake layout of the J-7 and this intake contained a large centrebody radome on the J-8I 'Finback-A' all-weather fighter variant. Production eventually commenced in 1985 and around 100 aircraft were completed. The J-8II 'Finback-B' is a much improved air superiority and ground attack version with a new fire control system and avionics and increased carrying capacity for external armament. It is fitted with Guizhou WP-13A engines and the forward fuselage was redesigned with fuselage side air intakes allowing the aircraft to have a large radar nose. The J-8II was first flown on 12 June 1984 and Shenyang has also built prototypes of the F-8IIM (above), which is an improved export version with higher-thrust WP-13B engines and a modernised cockpit with a HUD and HOTAS controls.

F-8IIM
Powerplant: two Guizhou WP-13B turbojets each rated at 68.70 kN (15,432 lb st) with afterburning

Performance: max speed 1300 km/h (808 mph), initial climb rate 13442 m (44,100 ft) per min, service ceiling 20200 m (66,275 ft), take-off run 670 m (2,200 ft), combat radius 800 km (497 miles)

Dimensions: wing span 9.35 m (30 ft 8 in), length 21.59 m (70 ft 10 in), height 5.41 m (17 ft 9 in)

Recognition features
A Delta wing
B Sharply-swept tail surfaces
C Long fuselage with tall engine air intakes behind cockpit

Sikorsky S-65 and S-80   *USA*

The S-65 was produced to a USMC requirement for an assault heli-copter, making its first flight on 14 October 1964. USMC aircraft were the CH-53A Sea Stallion, CH-53D and RH-53A mine sweeper. The USAF received the CH-53C transport and CSAR HH-53C Super Jolly. The MH-53J/K, in standards up to Pave Low IV, equipped for special forces insertion and CSAR, was also procured. Some 110 CH-53Gs were built by VFW-Fokker for the German army. The S-80 (CH-53E) Super Stallion is a triple-engined development with a seven-bladed main rotor, enlarged sponsons and a new tailplane. The mine countermeasures MH-53E Sea Dragon flies with the USN, the JMSDF (S-80M-1, right) and Taiwan. **Recognition features A** Multi-bladed main rotor **B** Podded engines **C** Large fuselage sponsons

Sikorsky S-70   *USA*

The S-70 won the 1972 US Army UTTAS competition and has been built for the US and for export. Its two GE T700 engines are mounted above the cabin. The prototype YUH-60A first flew on 17 October 1974. Numerous variants have included the UH-60A and UH-60L (right) Black Hawk, MH-60K special ops aircraft, EH-60A ECM helicopter, CSAR MH-60G Pave Hawk, VIP VH-60A and medevac UH-60Q. The S-70B (SH-60B) Seahawk naval version was designed to the LAMPS III specification and has also been widely exported. Versions include the USCG's HH-60J Jayhawk. **Recognition features A** Low, squat profile **B** Fixed tricycle undercarriage **C** Canted tail rotor

Sukhoi Su-24 'Fencer'   *Russia*

The Su-24 tactical bomber was first flown in June 1967. A major redesign resulted in the fitting of a variable-sweep wing and the new version first flew in May 1970 and subsequently entered service as the Su-24 'Fencer-A/B'. It is powered by a pair of afterburning AL-21F-3A turbojets positioned side-by-side in the rear fuselage. Surviving in-service Su-24s are based on the Su-24M 'Fencer-D' (right), with a retractable flight refuelling probe, a longer nose, overwing fences and new terrain-following radar. **Recognition features A** Wide, box-like fuselage **B** Huge lateral engine air intakes **C** Side-by-side cockpit

Sukhoi S-37/Su-47 Berkut   *Russia*

The Sukhoi OKB has developed the S-37 Berkut (golden eagle, above) as a highly agile single-seat experimental fighter prototype to test a variety of aerodynamic concepts. The most notable feature is the aircraft's forward swept wing, which is set well to the rear of the fuselage and blends into prominent wing leading edge fairings. The forward section of these fairings carries a canard surface with elevators, while provision is made in the left upper fairing for an internal 30-mm cannon. The S-37 is also fitted with rear tailplanes and twin fins. The two D-30F-6 afterburning turbofans do not have thrust vectoring nozzles, although this may be expected as a future change. Weapons are likely to be carried on external pylons, some sources suggesting that wing tip-mounted AAM rails may be employed, as might an internal weapons bay or semi-conformal missile carriage. The S-37 first flew on 25 September 1997 and testing is continuing. On 10 January 2002, the Russian government announced its intention to seek tenders for a fifth generation fighter. With some 90 test flights completed by that date, the S-37, since redesignated Su-47 Berkut, is likely to perform an important aerodynamic and technology proving role in Sukhoi's development of such a fighter. Sukhoi is seen as the manufacturer most likely to settle the requirement, with its design joining a light attack platform (possibly based on MiG-AT or Yak-130) and the Su-27IB as Russia's future front-line combat types.

S-37
Powerplant: two Aviadvigatel D-30F-6 turbofans each rated at 153 kN (34,392 lb st) with afterburning

Performance: max speed (estimated) 2200 km/h (1,367 mph), max speed at sea level (estimated) 1400 km/h (870 mph), service ceiling (estimated) 18000 m (59,060 ft), range (estimated) 3300 km (2,050 miles)

Dimensions: wing span 16.70 m (55 ft), length 22.60 m (74 ft), height 6.40 m (21 ft)

Recognition features
A Forward-swept wing
B Small, fixed horizontal tail surfaces
C Canards mounted at the shoulders of the intake trunks

Sukhoi Su-17, -20 and -22 'Fitter' *USSR*

The Su-17 'Fitter' was a derivative of the earlier Su-7 'Fitter-A' ground attack aircraft which was built in large numbers for the VVS and Warsaw Pact countries in the 1960s. The Su-7 was a single-seat aircraft with a highly swept low wing, tricycle undercarriage and a through-flow AL-7F-1 turbojet fed by a nose air intake. The Su-17 had a completely new wing with variable-sweep outer panels and detail changes including a deeper dorsal spine and a slightly longer forward fuselage. The prototype first flew on 2 August 1966 and first deliveries of the operational Su-17 'Fitter-C' took place in 1967, followed by the Su-17M 'Fitter-C' (Su-20 for export), which had a higher-powered AL-21F-3 engine. The 'Fitter' is normally equipped with nine pylons for bombs, rockets and missiles. Further variants included the Su-17M-2 (Su-22 'Fitter-F' for export) 'Fitter-D', Su-17M-3 'Fitter-H' (Su-22M 'Fitter-J' for export) with improved attack electronics and the redesigned forward fuselage of the Su-17UM 'Fitter-E' (Su-22U 'Fitter-G) trainer, and the final production Su-17M-4 'Fitter-K' (above) (Su-22M-4 'Fitter-K'), which has further avionics improvements and an air intake in the leading edge of its dorsal fin fairing. Many countries, including the Czech Republic, Libya, Peru, Syria and Vietnam, still operate 'Fitters'.

Su-22M-4 'Fitter-K'
Powerplant: one Saturn/Lyulka AL-21F-3 turbojet rated at 110.32 kN (24,802 lb st) with afterburning

Performance: max speed 1400 km/h (870 mph), initial climb rate 13716 m (45,000 ft) per min, combat radius 1150 km (715 miles)

Dimensions: wing span (spread) 13.79 m (45 ft 3 in), length 18.74 m (61 ft 6 in), height 5 m (16 ft 5 in)

Recognition features
A VG outer wing panels
B Pitot engine air intake with centrebody
C Large spine fairing cockpit into swept fin

Sukhoi Su-27 and Su-30 family   *Russia*

The Su-27 'Flanker' air superiority fighter first flew as the T-10-1 on 20 May 1977, but the production Su-27 was considerably modified with a new swept wing with prominent LERXes and changes to the tail unit and its AL-31F turbofans, which are positioned in the lower rear fuselage and fed by two large ventral air intakes. The Su-27 is fitted with a prominent retractable speed brake in the upper centre fuselage. The definitive Su-27 first flew on 20 April 1981. Other variants included the export Su-27SK and Su-27SMK. The Su-27UB (and export Su-27UBK) is a combat-capable tandem two-seat trainer with a raised rear cockpit, a common rear-hinged canopy and enlarged fins. This was also developed into the Su-30 (Su-30K for export) two-seat interceptor and Su-30M (Su-30MK for export, above) multi-role fighter. The Su-33 (Su-27K) is a carrierborne fighter version with folding wings and tailplane and modified leading edge extensions with additional canard control surfaces. Sukhoi has also flown the prototype of the Su-27KUB (Su-33UB), a naval trainer with a side-by-side two-seat cockpit. In addition, it has developed the advanced Su-35 multi-role fighter and the high-agility Su-37, which is fitted with thrust-vectoring engine nozzles and canards. The Su-30MKI for India is to be fitted to this standard.

Su-27 'Flanker-B'
Powerplant: two NPO Saturn AL-31F turbofans each rated at 122.60 kN (27,557 lb st) with afterburning

Performance: max speed 2500 km/h (1,554 mph), initial climb rate 18000 m (59,054 ft) per min, service ceiling 17700 m (58,071 ft), range 1400 km (875 miles)

Dimensions: wing span 14.71 m (48 ft 3 in), length 21.94 m (72 ft), height 5.94 m (19 ft 6 in)

Recognition features
A Long forward fuselage with large conical radome
B Tall twin fins
C Extended tailcone between engine nozzles

Sukhoi Su-32 and Su-34 *Russia*

The airframe of the Su-27 'Flanker' was used as the basis for the Su-27IB (later Su-34 (above) or Su-32 for export, although the Russian forces retained the Su-27IB designation) all-weather fighter bomber. The complete forward fuselage was modified to create a side-by-side two-seat cabin, accessed through a ventral hatch in the nosewheel well, and is large enough to contain a crew rest area, cooking facilities and a toilet. The forward fuselage also had the wing leading edge extensions running into ridged surfaces, extending to a flattened radar nose. The undercarriage has been redesigned with a rearward-retracting nosewheel and twin-wheel main bogies, and the tail sensor and countermeasures fairing have been substantially enlarged. The Su-34 designation has now been dropped, existing or proposed versions including the Su-27IB Interceptor, Su-27R recce aircraft, and Su-32FN/MF maritime strike and ASW aircraft. The Su-32 has 12 external hardpoints and is fitted with a GSh-301 single-barrelled 30-mm cannon. The prototype was first flown on 13 April 1990 and further development aircraft have flown, but the programme has been delayed by funding problems. It seems likely that the Russian air force will eventually adopt the Su-32 as its standard attack aircraft to replace the Su-24 'Fencer' and Su-25 'Frogfoot' in service.

Su-34

Powerplant: two Saturn/Lyulka AL-31F turbofans each rated at 137.30 kN (30,865 lb st) with afterburning

Performance: max speed 1900 km/h (1,181 mph), initial climb rate 16800 m (55,117 ft) per min, service ceiling 19800 m (65,000 ft), range 4000 km (2,500 miles)

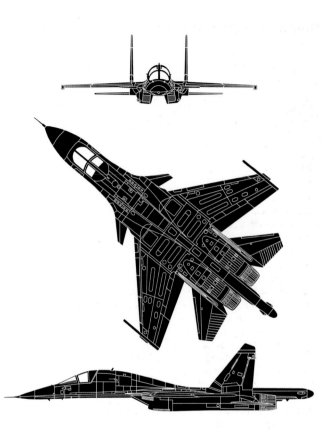

Dimensions: wing span 14.71 m (48 ft 3 in), length 23.29 m (76 ft 5 in), height 5.99 m (19 ft 8 in)

Recognition features
A Side-by side cockpit in 'platypus' forward fuselage
B Twin-wheel main undercarriage bogies
C Huge tail cone fairing

Tupolev Tu-22M 'Backfire'   *Russia*

The Tu-22M 'Backfire' medium bomber was developed as a follow on to the earlier Tu-22 'Blinder' which was designed as a replacement for the Tu-16. The Tu-22 and Tu-22M are substantially different, but retain the Tu-22 core designation. The Tu-22M prototype, which first flew on 30 August 1969, had swing wings with a substantial highly swept inner section incorporating large flaps and slim, tapered variable-sweep outer sections. It was powered by two reheated turbofans set side by side in the rear fuselage and fed by large, slightly angled variable intakes. The Tu-22M's tricycle undercarriage has six-wheel main bogies which retract inwards into the wingroots, and the nose section has a large radome for the attack radar and a cabin section with side-by-side seating for the two flight crew and a rear cabin for the navigator and communications specialist. Offensive stores are carried in a belly bomb bay with a rotary dispenser for up to six AS-16 'Kickback' tactical missiles, and on two pylons attached to the inner wing which can accommodate AS-4 'Kitchen' stand-off nuclear ASMs. The initial Tu-22M-1 'Backfire-A' went into production in 1969 but was quickly replaced by the Tu-22M-2 'Backfire-B', 211 of which were built before the Tu-22M-3 'Backfire-C' (above), with modernised systems, upgraded NK-25 engines and new raked air intake geometry, replaced it in 1976. It is thought that 280 'Backfire-Cs' were built. The Tu-22M is in front-line service with the Russian air force and navy and the Ukrainian air force. India is to sign a deal for the lease of a pair of Tu-22M-3s in 2002.

Tu-22M-3 'Backfire-C'
Powerplant: two Kuznetsov NK-25 turbofans each rated at 245 kN (55,115 lb st) with afterburning

Performance: max speed 2000 km/h (1,242 mph), initial climb rate (estimated) 5486 m (18,000 ft) per min, range 6760 km (4,225 miles)

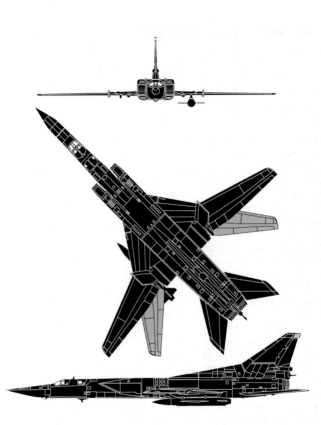

Dimensions: wing span (spread) 34.29 m (112 ft 6 in), length 42.47 m (139 ft 4 in), height 11.05 m (36 ft 3 in)

Recognition features

A Low-set, VG wing

B Large twin engines with huge raked lateral intakes

C Upturned nose on M-3

D Broad-chord fin and fairing

Sukhoi Su-25 'Frogfoot'   *Russia*

The Su-25 'Frogfoot' ground-attack aircraft first flew on 22 February 1975. It is a single-seater with a shoulder-mounted tapered wing and two Tumanski R-195 turbojets. It has been widely exported as the Su-25K (right). The Su-25UB 'Frogfoot-B' is a tandem two-seat trainer with a heavily-framed cockpit canopy. The Russian navy operates the Su-25UTG carrier-capable two-seater with folding wings, and an upgraded single-seat attack model, the Su-25T (known to Sukhoi as Su-39), has been developed with the rear cockpit enclosed and used for extra fuel tanks and avionics.

Recognition features A Engines mounted on fuselage sides **B** Straight wing with multiple pylons **C** Humpbacked appearance

Tupolev Tu-95/Tu-142 'Bear'   *Russia*

The Tu-95/Tu-142 'Bear' continues in front-line service despite having first flown on 12 November 1952. Its swept wing mounts four Kuznetsov NK-12M turboprops with counter-rotating propellers. The only bomber variant left is the Tu-95MS-6 'Bear-H', but the MS is based on the Tu-142 airframe, and the ASW Tu-142 remains in service with Russia and India (right) as the Tu-142 'Bear-F', with a lengthened forward fuselage, a strengthened wing, new radars and a prominent MAD tail stinger. The Tu-142MR 'Bear-J' version is also in Russian service as a strategic airborne communications relay and command post.

Recognition features A Swept wing **B** Four turboprop engines **C** Long, thin fuselage

Westland Sea King   *UK*

Based on the Sikorsky SH-3D, the ASW Sea King HAS.Mk 1 was powered by two Rolls-Royce Gnome H.1400 turboshafts, and had numerous other changes. The first HAS.Mk 1 flew for the first time on 7 May 1969 and later variants were the HAS.Mk 2; the RAF's SAR HAR.Mk 3 and Mk 3A; the HC.Mk 4 (Commando for export) assault helicopter; the HAS.Mk 5 and HAS.Mk 6; and the AEW.Mk 2A and Mk 7, with radar in an inflatable radome. Export Sea Kings are many, and include the Australian Mk 50A (right). **Recognition features A** Boat-like hull **B** Strut-braced sponsons **C** Five-bladed main rotor

Aviation as a Hobby

Aircraft are exciting! Next to computers, aviation is probably the technology which has most changed the world in the twentieth century. Airlife invites you to discover the Aviation Hobby – which provides a fascination to many millions of people around the globe.

Identifying different types of aircraft became important in World War I – and a matter of life and death in World War II. Britain, which was on the front line of wartime Luftwaffe attacks, set up spotting posts along its Channel Coast and this emphasis on 'spotting' continued after the war with the Royal Observer Corps – and is kept alive with the present-day hobby carried on by aircraft enthusiasts internationally. The aircraft spotting habit has expanded into a wide-ranging interest which includes aircraft recognition, collection of aircraft registrations, photography, research into aircraft production and the detailed study of aircraft and aviation history.

Aircraft Recognition

For the casual observer, one aircraft can be almost indistinguishable from another. The problem becomes more complicated rather than less as new aircraft types are added to our crowded skies. The number of types of aircraft has grown rapidly during the 1980s and 1990s and competing designers have often come up with very similar answers to particular specifications. Until one has mastered the art of aircraft recognition, a DC-10 and a TriStar can be easily confused – and separating a Saab Gripen from a Eurofighter or Dassault Rafale in a high-speed flying display can test even the most expert observer.

To become a recognition expert there is no substitute for experience. The enthusiast will quickly become conversant with different aircraft types by reading aviation magazines, visiting airports and going to airshows. However, there are some essential guidelines which will speed up the process of identification.

First impressions are always the most important. An aircraft flies overhead and one should be able to tell immediately whether it is large or small. Does it look like an airliner, a light aircraft, a helicopter, a military jet – or even a glider? Can you tell from from the noise it makes whether it is powered by jet or piston engines? These are judgements which nearly everyone can make and they immediately narrow down the range of possible answers. Sometimes, the solution comes easily. You can visit an airport where there are confusing rows of airliners – but many of them will have 'Boeing 777' or 'Airbus A 320' painted on the side, which solves the problem immediately.

Once the initial judgement is made, you can start to look at the general characteristics of the aircraft. Cast your eyes over its main components and mentally list its features.

The wings
- are they High, Mid or Low set on the fuselage?
- are there one (monoplane), two (biplane) or, maybe, three (triplane) sets of wings?
- are they straight wings, swept – or maybe delta-shaped?

The engines
- how many engines does the aircraft have?
- are they propeller-driven or jet engines?
- if there are two or more engines, are they mounted on the wings or on the fuselage?

The tail
- does it have a single fin – or two or three fins – or, maybe, a V-tail?
- is it swept back or 'straight'?
- does it have the tailplane positioned at the top, middle or the base?

The fuselage (the body of the aircraft)
- does it have a conventional fuselage or does it have twin booms?
- what kind of cabin does it have? A bubble cockpit, an open cockpit, or a large flight deck?
- is the rear fuselage continuous or upswept (perhaps with a cargo ramp)?
- are there cabin windows along the fuselage?
- what does the landing gear look like? Is it fixed or retractable, tricycle or tailwheel?
- if it is a military jet, where is the air intake – in the nose, flanking the cockpit area, etc?

If in doubt, write down your conclusions before you search through the pages of this book to find out which type you have seen. Your summary may say – 'Large airliner with swept back low wings, four engines fitted under the wings, tailplane attached to the fuselage and a retracting tricycle undercarriage'.

Or – 'Single-seat jet fighter with one engine and delta wings'. Or even – 'High-wing light aircraft with a single propeller-driven engine in the nose and a fixed tricycle undercarriage'.

This technique will allow you to eliminate the vast majority of aircraft – but it will leave you with a short list of types which look dauntingly similar. This is the point at which you have to get down to the fine differences leading to a correct identification. Do not worry if you cannot reach the answer immediately. Even experienced spotters find difficulty with, for instance, the wide-body Boeing 767 and Boeing 777 when seen at a distance. Here it is necessary to look very closely at the competing types and find the tiny differences. In the case of the wide-body Boeings, for instance, the '777 is larger than the '767 – but that may not be evident if you cannot see the two parked side-by-side! However, the '777 has a distinctive squared-off tail cone on its fuselage whereas the '767 tailcone is pointed – and the main undercarriage of the '777 has six wheels on each bogie, whereas the '767 has four.

Regrettably, even with this close scrutiny the enthusiast can come to the wrong conclusion. Most successful aircraft types are produced in different versions to meet various requirements. It is very common for airliner types to be 'stretched' so as to accommodate varying passenger loads. For instance, Boeing's highly successful '737 started out as the Model 100 with a 94-ft fuselage capable of carrying up to 101 passengers but has expanded to the 177-seat '737-900 which is 138-ft long. A useful distinguishing feature separating the Airbus A320 and the Boeing 737 was the winglets fitted to the Airbus; unfortunately, recent Boeing 737s have also had winglets added! So, the enthusiast has to accumulate experience and familiarity with all these aircraft – and also resort to a range of other methods of identification.

Aircraft Registrations

Both civil and military aircraft carry individual registration markings. In the case of civil aircraft these include a national identification consisting of one or two prefix letters which are issued by the International Civil Aviation Organisation (ICAO).

A full listing of these prefixes is given in Airlife's *Civil Aircraft Recognition*. The military authorities of each country also allocate their own serial numbers and use a system of distinctive national markings (which are shown in this book). Civil and military registrations for most countries in the world are given in a variety of commercially available directories which can be purchased by enthusiasts.

There are also annual volumes which concentrate on particular classes of aircraft – such as business jets, and there are many websites on the internet which can be accessed through index sites such as tgplanes or AirNet. Clearly, it is a simple matter to identify an aircraft's type by noting its registration and checking its details in one of these directories. In addition, many civil aircraft registers provide details of the owner of the aircraft, which adds to the interest of spotting the aircraft.

The directories also give details of the manufacturer's serial number (the 'construction number' or 'c/n') which gives a good idea of where the aircraft falls within the overall production of that model. The c/n is also useful for identifying an aircraft which has changed registration. This will happen when an aircraft is sold from one country to another and is allocated new markings by its new country of ownership.

Many aircraft enthusiasts keep a log of all the aircraft they have seen. It is, of course, impossible to see and log every aircraft in the world! So, most spotters concentrate on particular types or classes of aircraft with the objective of seeing and logging them all. One may collect business jets or airliners – or military aircraft. A pair of binoculars is very helpful – and a good notebook is essential. This can be a proprietary notebook such as *Airlife's Aircraft Logbook* or a simple lined notebook is more than adequate when ruled with columns showing the place and date seen, the registration and aircraft type. Other details may include the airline or operator and information on the colour scheme or special markings. Some spotters collect every different registration – and some are happy if they log a particular airframe irrespective of the registration it is carrying. The choice is an individual one.

Books and Magazines

The range of books and magazines is enormous and the only limitation is the size of your bank balance! Weekly magazines such as *Flight International* and *Aviation Week* cater primarily for those in the aviation industry while many monthly magazines are published for enthusiasts. These include *Aeroplane Monthly, Air Pictorial, Flypast, Pilot* and *Air International* in the UK and *Flying, Private Pilot* and *Air & Space* in the US. Books are available on almost every aviation subject and the large range of Airlife titles can be viewed and purchased at www.airlifebooks.com. We hope you enjoy discovering the exciting world of aircraft!

International Military Aircraft Markings

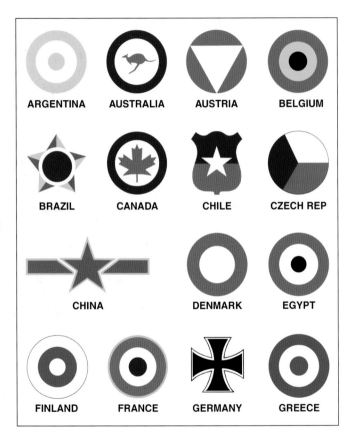

ARGENTINA AUSTRALIA AUSTRIA BELGIUM

BRAZIL CANADA CHILE CZECH REP

CHINA DENMARK EGYPT

FINLAND FRANCE GERMANY GREECE

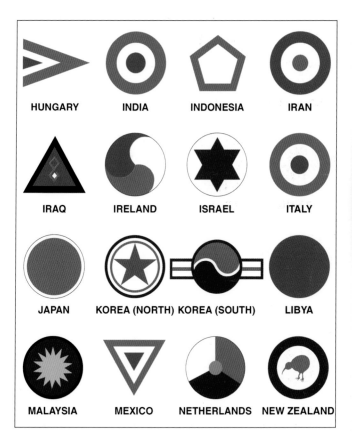

HUNGARY   INDIA   INDONESIA   IRAN

IRAQ   IRELAND   ISRAEL   ITALY

JAPAN   KOREA (NORTH)   KOREA (SOUTH)   LIBYA

MALAYSIA   MEXICO   NETHERLANDS   NEW ZEALAND

NORWAY PAKISTAN PARAGUAY PERU

PHILIPPINES POLAND PORTUGAL

ROMANIA RUSSIA (CIS) SAUDI ARABIA SINGAPORE

SLOVAKIA SLOVENIA SOUTH AFRICA SPAIN

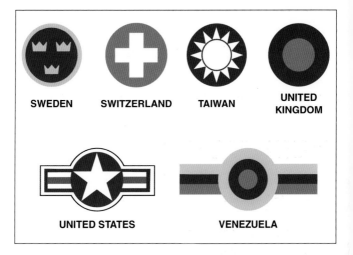

SWEDEN SWITZERLAND TAIWAN UNITED KINGDOM

UNITED STATES VENEZUELA

NATO Codenames

In 1954, the US Department of Defense introduced a system of code-names for Soviet aircraft. These were later adopted by the ASCC (Air Standards Coordinating Committee of the USA, UK, Canada, Australia and New Zealand) which continued to allocate names to new types until the mid-1990s when the correct design designations of most Russian aircraft became known. Sometimes referred to as NATO code-names, they were often suffixed with letters to identify sub-variants (e.g. Flagon-C) and fighters had names starting with F, bombers with B, transports with C, helicopters with H and training and other types with M. Chinese aircraft were also included briefly (e.g. Finback allotted to the Shenyang J-8). These codenames are still widely used although the correct designations are increasingly referred to in aviation publications.

ASCC Codenames for Warsaw Pact Aircraft

Name	Aircraft Designation
Backfire	Tupolev Tu-22M
Badger	Tupolev Tu-16
Badger	Xi'an H-6
Beagle	Ilyushin Il-28
Beagle	Harbin H-5
Bear	Tupolev Tu-95/Tu-142
Bison	Myasishchev 3MS-2
Blackjack	Tupolev Tu-160
Blinder	Tupolev Tu-22
Bounder	Myasishchev M-50/M-52
Brewer	Yakovlev Yak-28
Cab	Lisunov Li-2
Camber	Ilyushin Il-86
Camel	Tupolev Tu-104
Camp	Antonov An-8
Candid	Ilyushin Il-76
Careless	Tupolev Tu-154
Cash	Antonov An-28
Cat	Antonov An-10

Name	Aircraft Designation
Charger	Tupolev Tu-144
Clank	Antonov An-30
Classic	Ilyushin Il-62
Cleat	Tupolev Tu-114
Cline	Antonov An-32
Clobber	Yakovlev Yak-42
Clod	Antonov An-14 Pchelka
Coach	Ilyushin Il-12
Coaler	Antonov An-72/-74
Cock	Antonov An-22 Antei
Codling	Yakovlev Yak-40
Coke	Antonov An-24
Colt	Antonov (PZL) An-29
Condor	Antonov An-124
Cookpot	Tupolev Tu-124 Ruslan
Coot	Ilyushin 11-18 Il-20/Il-24
Cossack	Antonov An-225 Mriya
Crate	Ilyushin Il-14
Creek	Yakovlev Yak-12
Crusty	Tupolev Tu-134
Cub	Antonov An-12
Cuff	Beriev Be-30/Be-32
Curl	Antonov An-26
Faceplate	Mikoyan Ye-5
Fagot	Mikoyan MiG-15
Farmer	Mikoyan MiG-19
Fencer	Sukhoi Su-24
Fiddler	Tupolev Tu-128
Finback	Shenyang J-8
Firebar	Yakovlev Yak-28PM
Fishbed	Mikoyan MiG-21
Fishpot	Sukhoi Su-9/Su-11
Fitter	Sukhoi Su-17/Su-20/Su-22
Flagon	Sukhoi Su-15
Flanker	Sukhoi Su-27
Flipper	Mikoyan Ye-152
Flogger	Mikoyan MiG-23/MiG-27
Forger	Yakovlev Yak-38
Foxbat	Mikoyan MiG-25
Foxhound	Mikoyan MiG-31
Freehand	Yakovlev Yak-36
Freestyle	Yakovlev Yak-141

Name	Aircraft Designation
Fresco	Mikoyan MiG-17
Frogfoot	Sukhoi Su-25/Su-28/Su-39
Fulcrum	Mikoyan MiG-29
Halo	Mil Mi-26/Mi-27
Hare	Mil Mi-1
Harke	Mil Mi-10
Havoc	Mil Mi-28
Haze	Mil Mi-14
Helix	Kamov Ka-27/Ka-28/Ka-32
Hermit	Mil Mi-34
Hind	Mil Mi-24/Mi-25/Mi-35
Hip	Mil Mi-8/Mi-9/Mi-17
Hokum	Kamov Ka-50/Ka-52
Homer	Mil V12
Hoodlum	Kamov Ka-126/Ka-128
Hook	Mil Mi-6/Mi-22
Hoop	Kamov Ka-22
Hoplite	Mil (PZL) Mi-2
Hormone	Kamov Ka-25
Hound	Mil Mi-4
Madcap	Antonov An-71
Madge	Beriev Be-6
Maestro	Yakovlev Yak-28U
Mail	Beriev B-12
Mainstay	Beriev A-50/Be-976
Magnum	Yakovlev Yak-30
Mallow	Beriev B-10
Mandrake	Yakovlev Yak-25RV
Mangrove	Yakovlev Yak-27
Mantis	Yakovlev Yak-32
Mascot	Ilyushin Il-28U
Max	Yakovlev Yak-18
Maxdome	Ilyushin Il-80/Il-87
May	Ilyushin Il-38
Maya	Aero L-29 Delphin
Mermaid	Beriev A-40
Midas	Ilyushin Il-78
Midget	Mikoyan MiG-15UTI
Mongol	Mikoyan MiG-21U
Moose	Yakovlev Yak-11
Moss	Tupolev Tu-126
Mule	Polikarpov Po-2
Mystic	Myasishchev M-17/M-55

United States Air Force Unit and Base Codes

Current USAF aircraft generally carry prominent two-letter tail code markings. These are primarily intended to identify the Wing or Group which operates the aircraft but, in practice, the codes relate to the home base used by that Wing. The codes themselves often consist of an abbreviation of the base airfield (e.g. DM for 355th Wing at Davis Monthan AFB). Sometimes, a Wing will detach a Squadron or specialised unit to another base in which case the aircraft continues to carry the code for its parent Wing and home base.

Code	Wing/Unit	Base
AC	177th FW	Atlantic City AP, NJ
AK	3rd Wing	Elmendorf AFB, AK
AK	3rd Wing	Anchorage AP, AK
AK	3rd Wing	Eielson AFB, AK
AL	187th FW	Montgomery AP, AL
AV	31st FW	Aviano AFB, Italy
AZ	162nd FW	Tucson AP, AZ
BB	9th RW	Beale AFB, CA
BC	110th FW	Battle Creek AP, MI
BD	917th Wing	Barksdale AFB, LA
CA	129th RQW	Moffett Field, CA
CB	14th FTW	Colombus AFB, MS
CC	27th FW	Cannon AFB, NM
CO	140th Wing	Buckley ANGB, CO
CT	103rd FW	Bradley AP, CT
DC	113th Wing	Andrews AFB, MD
DM	355th Wing	Davis Monthan AFB, AZ
DY	7th BW	Dyess AFB, TX
ED	412nd TW	Edwards AFB, CA

Code	Wing/Unit	Base
EF	147th FW	Ellington, TX
EG	33rd FW	Eglin AFB, FL
EL	28th BW	Ellsworth AFB, SD
ET	46th TW	Eglin AFB, FL
FC	336th TG	Fairchild AFB, WA
FE	90th SPW	Francis E Warren AFB, WY
FF	1st FW	Langley AFB, VA
FL	920th RQG	Patrick AFB, FL
FM	482nd FW	Homestead AFB, FL
FS	188th FW	Fort Smith AP, AR
FT	23rd FG	Pope AFB, NC
FW	122nd FW	Fort Wayne AP, IN
GA	116th BW	Savannah AP, GA
HH	154th Wing	Hickam AFB, HI
HL	388th FW	Hill AFB, HI
HT, HO	46/49th TG	Holloman AFB, NM
HV	30th SPW	Vandenberg AFB, CA
ID	124th FW	Boise AP, ID
IL	182nd AW	Peoria AP, IL
IS	85th Gp.	Keflavik, Iceland
KS	81st TG	Keesler AFB, MS
LA	2nd BW	Barksdale AFB, LA
LD	IAAFA	Kelly AFB, TX
LF	56th FW	Luke AFB, AZ
LN	48th FW	RAF Lakenheath, UK
LR	944th FW	Luke AFB, AZ
MA	102nd FW	Barnes AP, MA

Code	Wing/Unit	Base
MD	175th FW	Warfield ANGB, MD
MI	127th FW	Selfridge ANGB, MI
MM	341st SPW	Malmstrom AFB, MT
MN	133rd AW	Minneapolis AP, MN
MO	366th AW	Mountain Home AFB, ID
MT	54th RQF	Grand Forks, ND
MT	5th BW	Minot AFB, ND
MY	347th Wing	Moody AFB, GA
NL	366th OG	NAS Whidbey Is., WA
NM	150th FW	Kirtland AFB, NM
NO, JZ	926th FW	NAS New Orleans, LA
NY	174th FW	Syracuse AP, NY
OF	55th Wing	Offut AFB, NE
OH	178/180th FW	Springfield AP, OH
OK	552nd ACW	Tinker AFB, OK
OK	138th FW	Tulsa AP, OK
OS	51st FW	Osan AB, Korea
PD	939th RQW	Portland AP, OR
RA	12th FTW	Randolph AFB, TX
RG	78th ABW	Robins AFB, GA
RI	143rd AW	Quonsett AP, RI
RS	37th AS	Ramstein AB, Germany
SA	149th FW	Kelly AFB, TX
SI	183rd FW	Springfield AP, IL
SJ	4th FW	Seymour Johnson AFB, NC
SP	52nd FW	Spangdahlem AB, Germany
SW	20th FW	Shaw AFB, SC

Code	Wing/Unit	Base
TD, TY	325th FW	Tyndall AFB, FL
TF, TX	301st FW	NAS Fort Worth, TX
TH	181st FW	Hulman AP, IN
TO	53rd Wing	Nellis/Holloman
VA	192nd FW	Richmond AP, VA
WA	57th Wing	Nellis AFB, NV
WE	53rd Wing	Tyndall AFB, FL
WG	913rd Wing	NAS Willow Grove, PA
WI	115th FW	Dane County AP, WI
WM	509th BW	Whiteman AFB, MO
WP	8th FW	Kunsan AFB, Korea
WR	93rd ACW	Warner Robins AFB, GA
WV	130th AW	Eastern Regional AP, WV
WW	35th FW	Misawa AFB, Japan
XL	47th FTW	Laughlin AFB, TX
XP	139th AW	Rosecrans AP, MO
YJ	36th AS	Yokota AB, Japan
ZZ	18th Wing	Kadena AFB, Japan

Abbreviations

ABW	Air Base Wing
ACW	Air Control Wing
AS	Airlift Squadron
AW	Airlift Wing
BW	Bomb Wing
FTW	Flying Training Wing
FW	Fighter Wing
RQG	Rescue Group
RQW	Rescue Wing
RW	Reconnaissance Wing
SPW	Special Purposes Wing
TG	Training Group
TW	Test Wing

Glossary of Aviation Abbreviations

AD	Airworthiness Directive
ADF	Automatic Direction Finding
AEW	Airborne Early Warning
AFB	Air Force Base
AFRes	Air Force Reserve (USA)
ALAT	French Army Aviation
ALPA	Airline Pilots Association
AMRAAM	Advanced Medium Range Air to Air Missile
ANG	Air National Guard (USA)
AOP	Air Observation Post
APU	Auxiliary Power Unit
ASI	Air Speed Indicator
ATC	Approved Type Certificate
ATC	Air Traffic Control
ATIS	Air Traffic Information service
AV-MF	Russian Naval Aviation
AWACS	Airborne Early Warning and Control System
BAA	British Airports Authority
BV	Bureau Veritas
CAA	Civil Aviation Authority
CAVOK	Cloud and Visibility OK
COIN	Counter Insurgency
CTA	Control Area
c/n	Construction Number
DEFCON	Defence Readiness Conditions
DME	Distance Measuring Equipment
DoD	Department of Defense (USA)
DoT	Department of Transportation (USA)
EAA	Experimental Aircraft Association
ECM	Electronic Counter-Measures
EFIS	Electronic Flight Instrumentation System
Elint	Electronic Intelligence
ELT	Emergency Locator Transmitter
ESM	Electronic Support Measures
ETA	Estimated Time of Arrival
ETD	Estimate Time of Departure

ETOPS	Extended-range Twin-engined Operations
FAA	Federation Aviation Administration (UK)
FAC	Forward Air Control
FADEC	Full-Authority Digital Engine Control
FAI	Fédération Aeronautique International
FBO	Fixed Base Operator
FBW	Fly-By-Wire
FLIR	Forward-Looking Infra-Red
GA	General Aviation
GCA	Ground Control Approach
GMT	Greenwich Mean Time
GPS	Global Positioning System
HOTAS	Hands on Throttle and Stick
HUD	Head-Up Display
IATA	International Air Transport Association
ICAO	International Civil Aviation Organisation
IFF	Identification Friend or Foe
IFR	Instrument Flight Rules
ILS	Instrument Landing System
IMC	Instrument Meteorological Conditions
INS	Inertial Navigation System
ISA	International Standard Atmosphere
JAR	Joint Airworthiness Requirements
JASDF	Japan Air Self Defence Force
JATO	Jet-Assisted Takeoff
LERXes	Leading Edge Root Extension
MAC	Military Airlift Command (USA)
MAD	Magnetic Anomaly Detector
MFD	Multi-Functional Display
MLU	Mid Life Update
MSA	Minimum Safe Altitude
MSL	Mean Sea Level
NASA	National Aeronautics & Space Administration
NATO	North Atlantic Treaty Organisation
NDB	Non-Directional Radio Beacon
nm	Nautical Mile
NORAD	North American Air Defense Command
NOTAM	Notice to Airmen
NOTAR	No Tail Rotor

NTSB	National Transportation Safety Board (USA)
OKB	Opytno Konstrooktorskoye Byuro
PAPI	Precision Approach Path Indicator
PAR	Precision Approach Radar
POC	Proof of Concept
QNH	Altimeter setting above MSL
RAAF	Royal Australian Air Force
RAF	Royal Air Force
SAR	Search and Rescue
SELCAL	Selective Calling
SLAR	Sideways-Looking Airborne Radar
SST	Supersonic Transport
STC	Supplemental Type Certificate
STOL	Short Takeoff and Landing
TACAN	Tactical Air Navigation Aid
TARPS	Tactical Air Reconnaissance Pod System
TAS	True Airspeed
TBO	Time Between Overhauls
TC	Type Certificate (USA)
TIALD	Thermal Imaging and Laser Designation
TMA	Terminal Control Area
TOGW	Takeoff Gross Weight
TORA	Takeoff Run Available
UAV	Unmanned Air Vehicle
UHF	Ultra High Frequency (radio)
ULM	Powered Ultra-Light Aircraft (French)
USAF	United States Air Force
USCG	United States Coast Guard
USMC	United States Marine Corps
USN	United States Navy
UTC	Coordinated Universal Time
VASI	Visual Approach Slope Indicator
VFR	Visual Flight Rules
VHF	Very High Frequency
VMC	Visual Flight Rules
VOR	VHF Omni-directional Range
VSTOL	Vertical/Short Takeoff and Landing
VTOL	Vertical Takeoff and Landing